A NEW INVITATION TO LINGUISTICS

JOSEPH H. GREENBERG is one of America's most distinguished linguists. He is a professor of anthropology at Stanford University and was formerly chairman of the Anthropology Department there. Professor Greenberg received a A.B. from Columbia University and a Ph.D. in anthropology from Northwestern University. In 1965 he became the first modern linguist to be elected to the National Academy of Sciences. He is also a member of the American Academy of Arts and Sciences and the American Philosophical Society. Professor Greenberg is currently president of the Linguistic Society of America. He is the author of seven books and of numerous articles.

JOSEPH H. GREENBERG

A NEW INVITATION
TO
Linguistics

ANCHOR BOOKS
ANCHOR PRESS/DOUBLEDAY
GARDEN CITY, NEW YORK
1977

Table in Appendix B adapted from *Aspects of Language*, 2d ed., by Dwight Bolinger. Copyright © 1968, 1975 by Harcourt Brace Jovanovich, Inc., and reprinted with their permission.

ISBN: 0-385-07550-2
Library of Congress Catalog Card Number 76-42422
Copyright © 1977 by JOSEPH H. GREENBERG
All Rights Reserved
Printed in the United States of America
First Edition

CONTENTS

PREFACE

It has been said that art is a kind of "distancing." The poet or painter stands back, as it were, and views with fresh insight and renewed wonder an object which we have come to take for granted as part of our everyday experience. Science, too, in its own and very different way, can accomplish something of this sort. The physical object which appears to be so solid to ordinary perception, is revealed as consisting of inconceivably small particles separated by spaces relatively so vast that if transposed to an astronomical scale, the solar system would seem, by comparison, to be packed with matter.

Language, too, is a subject—or object—of wonder. In our ordinary daily round we employ it thousands of times a day. We live as if bathed in a sea of words. Hence, like other familiar things, we take it for granted. Yet it is indeed a thing to be wondered at that human beings, of all creatures, by a series of minute anatomical adjustments produce a huge variety of sounds organized into those intricate structures we call languages.

So focal has language become, as part of the human experience, that we cannot imagine what it would be like not to have it. Our very thoughts about such a condition require the use of language in order to express them.

The world of the prelinguistic child and animals is to us a silent abyss into which we can no longer descend. We know that intelligent behavior occurs at the prelinguistic level, but we cannot conceive of what it really is like.

Language is so rich and complex that it can be approached from many points of view. Since it is possible to touch on only some of these in this book, we will concentrate on the nature of language as organized structure and the relation of language as a fundamental human institution to other institutions characteristic of human beings as they live in organized groups.

To understand better the distinction between these two points of view, let's think of language as a code. Indeed, spoken language can be transposed into a written form and this form itself made the basis of a code in the usual sense. To learn to use such a code is in a way like learning a game. Like a game, it has its rules, but they are of a much higher level of complexity than those of even the most complicated board games.

Moreover, no normal human being learns the rules of this game by explicit instruction, at least for his first and native language. There is no rule book for prelinguists to which he can turn. For such rules would themselves have to be codified in linguistic form. His parents will be as unaware of these rules and unable to formulate them as the child who acquires them. It is an amazing achievement on the part of the child that in a short time he masters and unconsciously follows the rules of a game thousands of times more complicated than chess.

The nature of this code as a set of rules on the one hand and a functioning social institution on the other are then two separate topics. They are, of course, related in a number of ways. To fulfill their social and cultural functions, all human languages must, as codes, have certain structural properties. For example, all languages must provide a vocabulary for the thousands of items that humans deal with even in the simplest societies. Moreover, all codes have the built-in flexibility by which new vocabulary items can be formed from old ones as nonlinguistic culture changes.

With this distinction in mind, we will, in the following pages, look first at the code properties of human language and, second, at language in its social and cultural context. We will not only acquaint the reader with some of the basic problems and concepts involved in the study of language but also, we hope, stimulate him to explore further the most essentially human of all attributes, articulate speech.

Chapter 1

THE NATURE OF LINGUISTICS

Neither science nor art can completely ignore linguistics. Every science, including linguistics itself, must pay some attention to its own terminology and the language in which it states its results. This inevitably involves problems of linguistic meaning and grammatical structure. In some disciplines the interest extends further. At the very heart of legal science lies such problems of semantic interpretation as the meaning of statutes and judicial decisions and the intention of legislators as expressed in the laws they pass. Preoccupation with linguistic matters is even more necessary to philosophy, which is today largely concerned with the linguistic analysis of philosophical concepts and statements. In the last decades the question regarding philosophical statements has shifted from "It is true?" to "What, if anything, does it signify?"

The concern with language is even more fundamental to the study of literature. Since the very material of prose and poetry is language, it has become widely accepted among students of literature that a systematic study of the linguistic basis of literature is fundamental to their work. This is especially necessary when the literature studied is not in the students' own native language.

However, these disciplines and many others are concerned with language as a means to some other end. The only science that is interested in language as an end in itself is linguistics, which takes its name from "language."

It would seem natural, at the very beginning, to define the object of our study, language itself. However, for the moment we will assume that what we mean is the set of entities such as English, Russian, Malay, and Swahili. Later we will take up the important questions of (1) what distinguishes such "natural languages" from a variety of other structures, such as animal communication, the "language" of mathematics, and even music, and (2) what is the basis for stating that as a communication medium, language is a unique and central human possession. These questions will be easier to comprehend and answer once we have considered various aspects of linguistics itself.

We will not, however, even at this point, take the notion of natural language entirely for granted. To begin with, it is important to distinguish clearly between language in its spoken and its written forms. While the linguist by no means disregards the written form, he considers the spoken form to be his primary object of study.

This runs counter to nonprofessional views which, if anything, tend to assign priority to writing over speech. It is important, therefore, to understand the reasons for the opposite assumptions shared by all linguists. First, speech comes first in the history of both the race and the individual. Human language goes back at least 100,000 years, while the first system of writing appeared only 5,000 years ago in Ancient Egypt. Every individual learns to speak before he learns to write. Every writing system is meant to represent some spoken language, but both in the past and present many forms of speech have no corresponding written form. Hence a science restricted to the latter would be extremely limited in scope.

An even more important reason involves linguistic change. The sounds of language are never completely stable over an extended period of time. When they change, the manner in which they do this can be understood from the physiology of the human sound-production mechanism. For example, in many languages, including the early form of Germanic from which English and the other present-day Germanic languages descend, an earlier *d* sound was replaced by *t*. These two sounds are the same except that the vocal chords vibrate in the former, or "voiced," sound and do not in the latter, which is therefore called "unvoiced." On the other hand, in the alphabet used by the speakers of Aramaic, a Semitic language, the written symbols for *r* and *d* became the same. This, of course, had no effect on the pronunciation. In time, *r* and *d* were distinguished by putting a dot under the letter for the former and over it for the latter.

A basically similar writing system can be used for many languages, whether related or not. In the past, writing generally spread with religion. Hence countries proselytized by Western Christianity generally use the Latin alphabet, those by Eastern Orthodox Christianity by an alphabet called Cyrillic, which is based on Greek, while most Islamic countries use the Arabic alphabet in some form. A language can be written with several systems of writing and still be the same language. The Serbs and Croats speak virtually identical languages, but the former who are Greek Orthodox use the Cyrillic alphabet while the latter who are Roman Catholic use the Latin. After World War I, the Turks, who up to that time had used the Arabic alphabet, switched to the Latin, but in no essential way changed the spoken (non-Arabic) language.

All this does not mean that the linguist considers writing unimportant or that it does not enter into his work in a number of ways. For example, the only knowledge we have of languages of the past is through written records. Hence the historical linguist must learn how to use the written form as evidence for the earlier spoken form. Still, his slogan is: "Better one live Babylonian (unfortunately not obtainable) than a thousand cuneiform tablets." Writing also exercises a minor influence on speech pronunciations, as when people introduce a *t* in the spoken word "often" because of its spelling. Such phenomena, however, are relatively rare and marginal compared with the importance of the spoken form in historical change.

One further preliminary remark is in order before we go on to consider linguistics in greater detail. The term "linguist" is often used by nonprofessionals to mean someone with a practical command of a number of languages. While some professional linguists do have such abilities, some of the most eminent have not. On the other hand, a nonprofessional linguist's ability to learn languages does not contribute to our scientific knowledge of language. For this reason, one professional linguist suggested that the term "linguistician" should be used for the scientific linguist, a suggestion that was never adopted. Something should also be said about the word "linguistics" itself. The term "philology" was formerly used for the scientific study of language, but is now obsolete in this sense, having become specialized to mean the linguistic study and interpretation of *written* texts. Of course, certain professional linguists interested in historical studies must understand the principles of textual criticism that they have in common with philologists. But, as we have seen, their interest focuses on a knowledge of the texts as evidence of the nature of the language rather than on a knowledge of the language to understand the text.

Like other sciences, linguistics has certain subdivisions, and all linguists are to a greater or lesser extent specialists. The differences in training of linguists and in their background in related sciences vary considerably. For this reason, besides general linguistic journals, there are numerous specialized journals for subdisciplines, which may also have their own separate international organizations and congresses.

Traditionally, the most basic division has been between historical and descriptive linguistics. Like many other fields, and in particular psychology and the social sciences, linguistics in its recognizably modern form is a nineteenth-century product. This is not to say that nothing of importance preceded or that the nineteenth century did not build on earlier achievements. However, the development of linguistics as a distinct discipline, in principle covering all languages, with a distinct and explicit goal and methodology is a nineteenth-century phenomenon. In particular, the intellectually exciting discovery was that languages which today differ from each other as much as English, Russian, and Persian could be differentiated descendants of a single, older language. This not only opened up new perspectives regarding prehistoric times but also led to the development of a distinct set of methods, known as "comparative linguistics." Thus these languages along with many others in Europe and Asia were found to belong to the family of languages called "Indo-European" and their hypothesized ancestral language was called Proto-Indo-European. By applying the comparative method, it was possible in large measure to reconstruct the linguistic features of Proto-Indo-European and trace its subsequent changes down to the contemporary languages. Linguistics in the nineteenth century was largely devoted to this enterprise and hence was historical in orientation and interested in the problem of change. The majority of nineteenth-century linguists were interested specifically in Indo-European languages, the family of languages which included those spoken by most of the professional linguists themselves. These studies centered largely in Germany. Some specialists also studied language families other than Indo-European, such as the Semitic languages, which include Hebrew and Arabic, or the Finno-Ugric group, which contains Finnish, Esthonian, Hungarian, and many other languages spoken further east.

Another important nineteenth-century development was that of phonetics as a kind of subscience of linguistics. At first, interest concentrated on the physiological basis of articulation, which laid the foundations for what is still the common way of classifying speech sounds. Toward the end of the nineteenth century there developed a second approach, laboratory phonetics, which uses instruments to analyze the physical basis of speech as displayed in sound waves.

A further development in the latter part of the nineteenth century was that of dialectology. Linguists began to realize that if they were to understand how languages had changed in the past, it was important to study change in contemporary speech—in particular, the kind of regional variations known as "geographical dialects"—since this process underlay the splitting up of language in the past. Hence they began systematic recordings and mappings of the local forms of languages like French, German, and Italian. The results were typically embodied in vast, detailed publications known as "dialect atlases."

This interest in contemporary speech and its variations, while arising from the historical interest that was natural in

the nineteenth century, was one of the important factors leading to the basic shift in theoretical interests that marks
twentieth-century linguistics—an interest in the structure of
language as it exists at a particular time, without regard to its
historical origins.

A second reason for the rise of structuralism, as this was
called, was the increasing concern with the languages of
non-Western areas, such as Africa and Asia. These partly
reflected the practical exigencies of missionary proselytization
and colonial administration but also partly the growing science of anthropology with its concern for non-Western and
"primitive" peoples—essentially those with simple technologies
and without systems of writing. Such languages could not be
studied easily by the methods of historical linguistics, which
largely relied on data from languages with written records
often extending back to remote periods of time. Also, the
models for grammatical description based on Western European linguistic tradition were found to be inadequate for the
analysis of forms of speech that were often utterly different
in structures.

Such considerations led linguists to concentrate on describing structures of languages without regard to their historical
antecedents and to the rise in linguistic theory of various
"structuralist schools" both in Europe and the United States.
The great pioneer of structuralism was the French Swiss linguist Ferdinand de Saussure (1857–1913), who taught at
Geneva and whose lectures were posthumously published by
his students in 1916 under the title *Cours de linguistique
générale.* This work has become the "Bible" of structuralism
not only in linguistics but in other fields for which the structuralist movement has contemporary significance—for example, anthropology and literary criticism.

De Saussure introduced the terms "synchronic" and "diachronic," which have since become theoretical terms of general currency in the historical and social sciences. By "synchrony," De Saussure meant the study of "states of language"
abstracted from time and in terms of the internal relations
of its elements, while by "diachrony" he meant the study of
change over time, which he viewed as a movement from ear-

lier to later states. He believed that the approaches of synchrony and diachrony were fundamentally so different that they should be the tasks of separate sciences.

While many did not follow him in advocating such a rigid separation, linguists since the rise of structuralism have viewed the main division of labor as being between those who continued the earlier tradition of historical linguistics and those who concerned themselves with linguistic structure without reference to historical factors.

There are many signs that this dichotomy is breaking down as linguists come to realize the intimate interconnection of these two approaches and the impossibility of studying one without regard to the other. Nevertheless, it remains an important basis of specialization, if only because the typical skills involved in training for these two areas are rather different.

In the last few decades a number of trends have developed, particularly in the United States, which have further broadened the scope of linguistics and added new specializations. Some of these are closely connected with the rise of a new and dominant school in world linguistics—the transformational approach to grammar associated with Noam Chomsky of the Massachusetts Institute of Technology, which first appeared in 1957 in his seminal work, *Syntactic Structures*.

Outside of its effects on linguistics proper, the work of the transformational school has been instrumental in developing certain barely touched-upon research areas into major specializations. One of these is the study of how children acquire language. Chomsky's idea that there was an innate apparatus of universal principles by which a child constructed a grammar of his or her language, although hotly disputed, provided the impulse for an enormous expansion of interest in this topic, one which, logically speaking, is a major subdivision of linguistics. Work in child language is carried out by psychologists with training in linguistics as well as by professional linguists and occasionally by the collaboration of both.

Their common interest is further evidenced in what has now become a major interdisciplinary pursuit, psycholinguistics. The central problem of psycholinguistics is that of the psychological reality of the grammatical rules posited by the linguists: How, if at all, do speakers actually use these rules in their behavior?

Transformationalists have also been at least partly responsible for the development of mathematical linguistics into another major subfield. Because transformationalists use formal methods to construct grammar—that is, manipulate abstract symbols according to certain rules—the methods themselves are subject to mathematical analysis. This has expanded into a major study of the mathematical and logical properties of codelike systems in general, of which natural languages are a special type.

At least one more field has recently grown into a major subdiscipline, but it is one whose major impetus has not been transformational theory. This is the study of sociolinguistics. As the name implies, it is also in principle an interdisciplinary field, but while it has generally involved linguists and some anthropologists, it has involved very few sociologists. The chief object of study in sociolinguistics is the functioning of language in society. It is a vigorously expanding field to which one of the later chapters of this book will be devoted.

Recent developments like these seem to indicate a period of varied and expanding interests that is perhaps the harbinger of a new and broader synthesis of the field. It is probable that a number of dogmas associated with by now traditional structuralism, and for the most part inherited by transformational theory, have outlived their usefulness. Among these are the separation of diachronic and synchronic linguistics and the structuralist emphasis on the latter as central to linguistic theory. To explain why in each case a given language has its particular structure requires the integration of diachronic factors of change into over-all theory. Another principle that has surely outlived its usefulness is the dichotomy between "language" and "speech"—"language" as an ideally uniform structure and the central subject matter of linguistics and "speech" as the actual variability in its use by individuals and social groups. Another major doctrine that has been associated with the linguistics of the last half century is the autonomy of linguistics. "Autonomy" in this context means that language should be investigated and explained only in terms of language itself and independent of logical, physiological, and sociocultural factors. This view, which was understandable and useful when linguistics was a fledgling science, has outlived its usefulness, and there are clear signs today of its weakening. What one hopes might eventuate is a multifaceted theory that will do justice to the existence and interconnection of the many aspects of language—as system, as historical product, and as an adaptation, both to the internal physical and mental endowments of human beings and to their external sociocultural environment.

Chapter 2

LANGUAGE AND STRUCTURE

It is remarkable that people are so unaware of the structure of the language they speak. Yet rules and relationships exist at every level of language, grammar, vocabulary, and sounds. Considering the complexity of the structure that governs our speech, uttering or understanding even a short sentence is a miracle and cannot be duplicated by the most sophisticated computer.

Consider, for example, the most frequently occurring English word, *the*. How many of us could explain to a Russian, who says, "I am happy to make acquaintance of your wife" when he should or should not use the definite article, *the*, with a noun in English? Yet, as native speakers of English, we choose without overt thought or hesitation, thousands of times each day, whether to put "the" before a noun or not.

As a first illustration of the concept of systematic structure, let's consider an important distinction among nouns that is rarely treated in school grammars. In English we have two articles—*the* and *a/an*—called the "definite" and "indefinite" articles respectively. Note, however, that in the singular three possibilities occur. A noun may be preceded by the definite article, the indefinite article, or no article at all, e.g., *the house, an orange, cheese*. In the plural, however, there is no indefinite article. Hence we can have *houses* and *the houses*, but not **a houses*.[1] There are thus five types of noun expres-

---

[1] The asterisk is a convention used in linguistics to indicate that the form that follows is hypothetical. The form may be one that is

sions in English: singular definite; singular indefinite; singular, no article; plural definite; and plural, no article. In Figure 1, below, these are indicated as follows: SD, SI, SNA, PD, and PNA.

If we examine the English nouns we find that they fall into two basic classes depending on which types of noun expressions they can form. We will take two nouns *house* and *sand* as representatives of these two classes. The expressions in which they can normally appear are marked with a plus sign and those with which they cannot with a minus sign.

		SD	SI	SNA	PD	PNA
A	sand	+	−	+	−	−
B	house	+	+	−	+	+

Figure 1.

The A class of nouns does not generally appear with the indefinite article, e.g., *a sand,* nor do they form plurals without altering their meaning. The B class on the other hand forms plurals but in the singular must as a rule take an article, whether definite or indefinite. A question such as "What is this?" illustrates the difference. The answer will be "A house," but "Sand." The A class consists of nouns representing things which cannot be counted and hence do not occur in the plural. The term used for them is "mass noun." The B class consists of nouns representing things which can be counted and hence do occur in the plural. They are called "count nouns."

Mass nouns sometimes occur in the plural, but if so, their meaning is usually different, either a poetic (e.g., *sands of time*) or the meaning "kinds of" (e.g., *cheeses*). The mass nouns cannot appear directly with numerals. They require an accompanying measure which itself takes the numeral and is, in fact, a count noun, e.g., *two pails of sand.* We might also distinguish a third class, abstracts, which behave very

derived through historical reconstruction but cannot be proved, or one that can be constructed from sounds or meaningful elements of the languages but do not exist in that language.

much like mass nouns. An example is *health*. We do not usually say "a health" or "two healths."

There are some nouns which are both count and mass nouns and therefore appear in all five kinds of expressions in Figure 1, e.g. *cake*. In such nouns there is a detectable difference of meanings between use in mass expressions, "I like cake," "Give me cake," and count expressions, "I bought five cakes," "There is a cake on the table."

These two major classes of nouns—mass and count—show a whole series of other characteristics. For example, there may be a difference in the words used with them to express certain indefinite quantities. Thus *much* goes with mass nouns and *many* with count nouns, as in "much cheese" but "many houses."

This example illustrates a further characteristic of structural analyses. The classes distinguished in one set of constructions—in this case, the use of articles—have a whole series of other distinctions in common, e.g., use of *much* as against *many*. This gives us confidence that our classification is significant in relation to the over-all structure of the language.

The foregoing analysis has acquainted us with two basic concepts of structure. Speech is a temporal succession of linguistic elements. In writing, this is mirrored in the linear sequence of letters and words. Such a sequence may, however, also be analyzed as consisting of *two* dimensions. First is the relation of successive items to each other, called the "syntagmatic" dimension. For example, in English, once we have an article, it must initiate a sequence called a noun phrase which always ends with a noun, e.g., *the large house, a very tasty and well-prepared dinner*. This sequential pattern is regulated in ways other than those already mentioned. For example, if there are several adjectives between the article and the noun, they fall into ordered classes. Thus adjectives denoting size and shape precede adjectives of color. We can say "a large red house" but not "a red large house."

These examples illustrate the second major dimension, that of a positional class. Such a class is a set of items which can potentially appear at the same place in the syntagmatic, or sequential, dimension. We used the term "potentially" because in any actual sentence only one member appears. The relation between members of a class is called the "paradigmatic" dimension. Figure 2 illustrates these two types of relationships. The dots in each column indicate that there are additional members not listed here.

Syntagmatic Relationships

Paradigmatic Relationships

this	very	large	red	house
that	quite	small	green	table
the	somewhat	circular	brown	•
a	•	•	•	•
one	•	•	•	•
•	•	•	•	•
•	•	•	•	•

Figure 2.

Such systems of syntagmatic and paradigmatic relationships occur at all levels, including that of sounds. Consider, for example, the different ways in which a word may begin in English. The initial sound may be a vowel as in *apple, eat, open;* it may also be a single consonant followed by a vowel as in *bad, carry, thin.* Since we are talking about sounds, not spelling, the *th* of *thin* counts as a single consonant. Further, some words begin with two consonants, for example, *stop, tree, swing.* The largest number of consonantal sounds with which an English word may begin is three, as in *string* or *square.* (The spelling is misleading in the latter case; the pronunciation involves an initial *skw* sequence.)

Now this is a systematic fact about English, which does not hold for languages in general. For example, there are languages like Spanish in which the maximum number is two and others like Hebrew which never allow more than a single consonantal sound to begin a word. There are still others, such as Russian, which allow longer sequences; the Russian *vzglad* 'a glance', has four consonantal sounds, which is the limit for Russian. Every language has a definite maximum, this being only one of a host of structural statements that can be made about a language.

Which sequences of three consonants occur? Is there any order or organization which we can discover from the words *spring, stream, scrape, split, sclerosis, square* (*skw*), *spew* (*spy*), and *skewed* (*sky*)? (The *y* here indicates the initial sound in *yard*.)

Well, the first element is always *s*. The table below, Figure 3, shows that in addition, every such initial sequence contains a member of the first set, a member of the second set and a member of the third set, and always in the order set forth in the table.

1	2	3
s	p	r
	t	l
	k	w
		y

Figure 3.

We see once more the two types of relationships. For example, *p* and *t* are in a paradigmatic relationship, while *s*, *t*, and *r* are in a syntagmatic relationship, as in the word *string*.

The members of the class in position 2—*p*, *t*, *k*—not only share the paradigmatic feature of functioning in the second place in initial consonant sequences, they also belong to the same phonetic set of consonants called "stops" because they involve a complete closing off of air in the mouth followed by an abrupt release. For this reason *p* is a stop sound; *f*, a sound which can be prolonged, is not. These stops also share the feature of voicelessness; that is, they are pronounced without vibration of the vocal chords. The voiced sounds which correspond to *p*, *t*, and *k* are *b*, *d*, and *g*, respectively. It turns out that *p*, *t*, and *k* are the only unvoiced stop sounds in English. An easy way to detect voicing is to put your fingers in your ears while you pronounce first *s* and then *z*. With the latter you can hear the buzzing sound produced by the vibration of the vocal chords.

The sounds in position 3—*r*, *l*, *w*, and *y*—once again show common characteristics, but different ones from those in position 2. These sounds are all voiced and they can be prolonged (i.e., they are not stop sounds). They are called "sonants," and, once again, the entire class so phonetically defined can function in this position.

In the examples above you probably noticed that to find an instance of *skl*, we had to resort to a somewhat unusual word, *sclerosis*. In fact this word is borrowed from the Greek. Since the *skl* fits well into the over-all pattern it is pronounced. But other initial consonant sequences in other words borrowed from Greek are not pronounced if they do not conform to the English structural scheme. For example *ptomaine* and *psalm*, both borrowed from Greek, are normally pronounced without the initial *p* sound. This shows that our structural observations have a certain explanatory power, and why we reproduce certain sound sequences and not others in words that are borrowed from another language.

Another example is that of the *-s* plural in English for nouns. From English spelling we might think that it has only two forms— *-s* as in *cup-s* and *-es* as in *church-es*. However, we often find a *z* sound, which is spelled with an *-s*, as in *log-s*. Further, the plural *-es* is actually a sequence consisting of a reduced vowel quite unlike the *e* in *set*, while the final *-s* is once more pronounced *z*. We will write this sequence as *əz*. There are then three different forms of the *-s* plural, namely, *-s*, *-z*, and *-əz*. What rule, if any, is there that determines our choice of one or the other alternative?

With *-s* we find instances like *cap-s*, *cat-s*, *rock-s*, *cliff-s*, and *myth-s*. Note that the *-th* sound of this last word is different from the *-th* of *lathe*. We will symbolize the first by the lower-case Greek letter θ (theta) and the second by ð (eth), a letter used in the writing system of Old English.

For the *-z* plural we have instances like *ribs*, *pads*, *logs*, *lathes*, *caves*, *hams*, *pans*, *rings*, *cars*, *wheels*, *sofas*, *pennies*. (Note that the two-letter sequence *-ng* designates a single sound. When we wish to refer to it, we will use the symbol ŋ.)

Finally, there are words whose plurals end in *-es*, which has the form *-əz*, as in *classes*, *sizes*, *dishes*, *mirages*, *churches*, *judges.* (Note that the form of the sound written *g,* as in *mirage,* is *ž;* of the *sh* of *dishes* is *š;* and of the *ch* of *church* is *č.*)

In every case the choice among -*s,* -*z,* and -*əz* is determined by the immediately preceding sound. Thus, given that we have -*z* in *rib-s,* we will expect that the same form will also occur in *tubs, Arabs,* etc. Hence, to arrive at a general rule we need only pay attention to the sound preceding the plural endings.

Using the symbols that have been introduced above, we may state the rule for plural nouns as follows:

1.   After *p, t, k, f,* and *θ,* we use -*s.*
2.   After *b, d, g, v, ð, m, n, ŋ, r, l,* and vowels, we use -*z.*
3.   After *s, š, z, ž, č,* and *j,* we have -*əz.*

The first set contains *p, t, k,* the members of the second set in the earlier rule regarding initial consonant sequences. This suggests that we look at the phonetic characteristics of each of the three sets of consonants above. The first set consists entirely of voiceless consonants; the second of voiced consonants; the third set, however, consists of both voiced and voiceless consonants, e.g., *s* is unvoiced, but *j* is voiced. However, all the sounds in the third group have one characteristic in common. They involve articulation in which the air rushes over a narrow (for *s, z*) or a wide (for *š* and *ž*) slit in the center of the tongue. Such consonants are called "sibilants."

Given this knowledge of phonetics we can now state the rules far more simply than before.

1.   The -*s* plural takes the form *s* after unvoiced sounds unless they are sibilants.
2.   The -*s* plural takes the form *z* after voiced sounds unless they are sibilants.
3.   The -*s* plural takes the form *əz* after sibilants.

This statement can be made still simpler. We can get rid of the clumsy proviso "unless they are sibilants" in the first two statements by ordering our rules. That is, if we first state that the choice is -*əz* if the preceding sound is a sibilant, we can then apply the following rules to the remaining consonants without further reference to the sibilants. Also, since -*s* is itself unvoiced and -z is voiced, we choose the form for the plural that agrees in voicing with the previous sound.

We can now state two very simple rules for plural nouns. First, if the previous sound is a sibilant, choose -əz. Second, if it is not, choose -s or -z, making it agree in voicing with the previous sound. As in the earlier example of the article with nouns, we are dealing with both paradigmatic relationships—in this case, the relations of sounds which exhibit the same properties in the choice of a plural form—and syntagmatic properties, e.g., that unvoiced sounds, unless sibilants, are followed by -s.

However, it differs from the previous example in two important ways. The syntagmatic relationship has an additional property. With regard to the choice between -s and -z, the plural suffix *agrees* in voicing with the last consonant of the stem.

Such regulation of choices among elements turns out to be a property of many syntagmatic relations. It may be called "agreement" and in fact it is usually called that on the grammatical level. For example, the verb subject agrees with the verb in English since each must choose either a singular or plural. There is number agreement in grammar just as there is voicing agreement in sounds in the above example.

The last two illustrations also differ in another important way. The rules concerning initial consonants apply exclusively to sounds. For the second, however, if we wish to make the rule complete, reference to sounds only is not sufficient. There are a small number of nouns in English which do not take -s plurals, for example, *ox, tooth, foot.* We cannot say that any noun ending in -ks has a plural in -en because the plurals of *box* and *fox* are not **boxen* and **foxen.* Hence, for a complete statement we need to go beyond the sounds. Such complex rules are common in language. A technical expression for them is "morphophonological" as against the purely phonological rules pertaining to initial consonant clusters.

One important aspect of language has not yet been discussed from the structural point of view. This is vocabulary. The vocabulary of a language is found in a dictionary, with every language containing thousands of words. They would seem at first to be a mass of isolated and disconnected items.

However, there are certain parts of the vocabulary that are highly systematic and the methods developed in this study are being applied to other more intractable lexical phenomena.

For example, we will consider just a part of the terminology used in English to classify relatives. Take, to begin with, the terms *father, mother, uncle,* and *aunt.* Disregard for the moment the use of the terms *aunt* for father's brother's wife or mother's brother's wife and of *uncle* as father's sister's husband or mother's sister's husband. The term *uncle* will then denote a father's or mother's brother and *aunt* a father's or mother's sister.

The two terms are obviously parallel in that both designate the sibling of either a father or a mother and only differ in regard to the sex of the person referred to. Another way of stating this is that in our terminology lineal relatives, that is, those in the direct line of descent, such as *father* or *mother* are distinguished from collateral relatives whether related through the mother (mother's brother, mother's sister) or through the father (father's brother, father's sister). Such relatives are called "matrilineal" and "patrilineal" respectively. Our system then distinguishes lineal from collateral relatives regardless of whether the latter are patrilineal or matrilineal both for males (father v. uncle) or females (mother v. aunt).

This lineal/collateral distinction runs through our whole kinship system. Children of the lineal relatives, i.e., father and mother, are brothers and sisters, but children of the collateral relatives, uncle and aunt, are cousins. Sons and daughters are distinguished from nephews and nieces, grandfather and grandmother from great-aunts and great-uncles, and so on.

This introduces a logical parallel to our earlier structural analysis of phonemes—the classification by features. Just as *p, t, k, f,* etc., are a class of sounds defined by voicelessness as against *b, d, g, v,* etc., as voiced, so father, mother, son, daughter, grandfather, grandmother, etc., are classified together as lineal as against uncle, aunt, nephew, niece, etc., which are collateral.

Further, just as every language has, as we have seen, certain rules about initial consonants each with its internal structure and consistency, so with kinship systems. As a matter of fact, only a minority of the world's languages make the lineal/collateral distinction fundamental, as it is in our system. A much more common system, for example, is that which operates in terms of lines of descent. Here the father and father's brother are designated by one term and the mother's brother, who is, of course, a matrilineal relative, by a second and different term. Such kinship terminologies invariably apply also to female relatives so that the matrilineal relatives, mother and mother's sister, are indicated by one term and the patrilineal relative, father's sister, by a different word. Once again, just as the terminology in our system shows structural consistency in distinguishing lineal from collateral relatives throughout, for these systems the difference between matrilineal and patrilineal relatives is applied throughout. For example, just as father and father's brother, have the same term, the children of father's brothers are called by the same terms as one's own brother and sister while one's mother's brother's children are addressed differently.

These examples could be multiplied a hundredfold for any human language. However, as fundamental and pervasive as such facts are, they are not a final explanation. We must also inquire why such structures exist and why particular languages have particular structures. Such questions will be taken up in the latter part of this book where we shall see that two basic approaches can be brought to bear on such problems. One approach is historical. Individual structures always have a history, and to explain them it is indispensable to understanding, among other factors, their past and how they have developed and changed over time.

The other key concept is type. Although every language exhibits a unique constellation of properties, for any particular aspect of the language, the structures involved are rarely confined to that particular language. Thus, in the discussion of kinship terminology, we found that some languages like English make a fundamental distinction between lineal and collateral relatives while others oppose patrilineal to matrilineal, the latter being distinctions based on the principle of descent, that is, through the father or the mother. In such systems, for example, the mother's brother and the father's brother have separate terms. There are still other types but very few in all. Therefore, many languages would in this respect belong to the same type.

If every language was a completely unique structure—that is, if types did not exist—the linguist would not be able to compare their structures. Hence, while he could say a great deal about individual languages, he could not develop theories about language as such, which is presumably the object of his science.

Finally, the examples discussed in this chapter represent three basic aspects of language—phonology, grammar, and semantics. While they are significantly interrelated, each seems to present certain special problems that require separate treatment and each can to a certain extent be studied on its own.

Of the three, only two might at first seem indispensable for any system of communication. The sign itself must take some physical form in a particular medium, most commonly visual or auditory. This is called the "sign vehicle." In natural language this corresponds to the sounds, and the study of the nature and functioning of the sounds is called "phonology." Secondly, it is of the very essence of signs that they communicate some meaning. The study of this aspect is "semantics." However, in a complex system such as language, there is a third aspect, namely, the rules regarding the arrangements and modifications of the signs themselves. This is what is generally called "grammar," although there is a wider use of the term "grammar" which includes all three aspects of language.

Grammar arises in natural language essentially because we speak in terms of complex structures we call "sentences." Sentences consist of combinations of meaningful elements (e.g., words) which take physical form (sounds). Every language has its own rules of sentence construction and to have adequate command of a language we must master its grammar as well as its phonology and vocabulary.

Consider the following simple example. Suppose I wish to say in German that my sister visited me yesterday. I must certainly know how to produce the sounds of German and I must know the vocabulary items that mean *my* ('mein'), *sister* ('Schwester'), *visit* ('besuchen'), *me* ('mich'), and *yes-*

terday ('gestern'). However if I simply say "Mein Schwester besuchen mich gestern," we will have a sort of pidgin German which will probably not be understood and will certainly not be the way in which a normal German speaker expresses this meaning. We may say, "Gestern hat meine Schwester mich besucht." Literally, 'Yesterday has my sister me visited'. The order of words will then be different in German and in English. Instead of a simple past like *visited,* the German tense system involves the use of a form corresponding to the English present perfect *has visited.* For *my,* one must consider a number of possible forms *mein, meiner, meine, meinen,* etc. whose choice depends on number (singular), case (e.g., subject as against object of the verb) and the membership of the word 'sister' in one of three gender classes, masculine, feminine, and neuter, which do not exist in English.

In the next few chapters we will consider each of these three fundamental aspects of language in turn and seek to develop in more detail and greater depth the principles whose acquaintance we have made in the present chapter.

Chapter 3

PHONETICS AND PHONOLOGY

So far we have used the word "phonology" in a very general way to mean the scientific study of the sound aspect of language. But now we must distinguish two levels of investigation. One is the purely physical or phonetic level, and the other is the phonological level at which we investigate the manner in which these sounds are organized into systematic structures in individual languages.

We can illustrate the difference between phonetics and phonology by the following example. Speakers of English think of the *t* sound as a unit and as one of the sounds of their language. On the purely physical or phonetic level, however, *t* is actually a set of distinct although similar sounds. For example, if we pronounce the word *take* and compare the *t* sound in this word with the *t* in *stop* and again in *put* we can perceive that these sounds are not all the same. The *t* of *take* has an audible puff of breath, somewhat like an *h* sound following it. This breathy quality is called "aspiration" by phoneticians. In phonetic transcription the *t* sound of *take* would be symbolized as [t']. Note that there is a convention that phonetic notations are included within brackets. On the other hand the *t* of *stop* would be symbolized as [t] since it has no such aspiration and hence in phonetic transcription would not be followed by the symbol for aspiration which is the reverse apostrophe [']. Finally, the *t* of *put* not only is not aspirated, but it is generally "nonreleased," that is, we do not end it with a sharp audible release of the closure which has been previously made. In this respect, it is unlike

both the *t* of *take* and that of *stop*. In fact there are still
other phonetically different varieties of the *t* sound in English
which need not be discussed here.

Now some readers may think that such differences are, after all, trivial and that all languages with *t* sounds will exhibit
similar "meaningless" variations. However, in many languages
t sounds which are similar respectively to the [t] of *stop* and
the [t'] of *take* occur but function differently. For example,
in Hindi a *t* like that of *stop* occurs in the word *tar* 'wet'
and one like that of *take* is found in the word *t'ar* 'den of
a wild beast'. In other words, these two sounds, which can
be identified phonetically with those of English, are capable
of distinguishing two different meanings, whereas in English
they are not. So on the phonetic level, English and Hindi are
similar, but on the phonological level they are not.

The distinct phonological units of sound structure are generally called "phonemes" and they are designated by writing
the symbol between slant lines instead of the brackets of phonetic transcription. Thus both English and Hindi have [t] and
[t'] phonetically, but English has only /t/ as a phoneme corresponding to these two sounds where Hindi has two different
phonemes, /t/ and /t'/ since in Hindi they contrast to produce different meanings but in English they do not.

The different phonetic varieties of /t/ in English never directly contrast with each other because the occurrence of each
variety is determined by rules. For example the unaspirated
variety always occurs after [s], the aspirated variety occurs
immediately before an accented vowel, provided that the [t']
is not preceded by an [s], etc. Since these variations are auto-
matic, speakers are not generally conscious of them.

With this distinction in mind, let's first consider the study
of phonetics, or speech sounds as such, and then take up the
manner in which speech sounds are organized into systems
on the phonological level.

All human beings have the same basic anatomical capabili-
ties and hence in principle any sound that can be produced
by one human being can be produced by another. We each
learn to make the sounds of the language that we acquired
in childhood. If we grew up in some other speech community,

we would acquire the sounds of this other community. This may seem self-evident, but there was a time when many people believed otherwise. Consequently, a universal basis for phonetics exists in human physiology. The same framework for describing and classifying speech sounds can be applied to all human languages.

The job of phonetics is to construct such a universal scheme through which any one of the enormous number of speech sounds capable of being produced and used in language anywhere can be classified and analyzed. Along with the analysis itself, there must be a system for recording the sounds—that is, a method of phonetic transcription that enables any trained investigator to record any sound he may encounter in the study of any human language.[1]

There are three conceivable bases for the classification of sounds. The first is articulation—that is, a description founded on the position and movements of the organs involved in producing sounds. The second is the analysis of the physical properties of the sound waves generated by the speech organs. The third is the acoustic impression produced in the hearer. The first of these, with a few exceptions, has become the basis for classifying speech sounds. For example, the b sound of English is called a "voiced bilabial stop" and the component terms are defined by reference to articulation. It is a sound produced by closure and abrupt release (stop) of the two lips (bilabial) and with the vocal chords vibrating (voiced).

There are a number of reasons for the priority accorded to articulation in the description and classification of speech sounds. Articulation is open to immediate observation. For this reason, it is, historically, the oldest method. Moreover, since no elaborate apparatus is required, it can be used by the linguist investigating a hitherto unrecorded language under field conditions. Such a linguist is trained to understand and control all the possibilities of articulation. Hence, when he hears a strange sound, he seeks to match it by his own articulation. He is then able to specify the articulations by which he has reproduced an acceptable imitation of the native sound

[1] For phonetic symbols used in this book, see Appendix A.

and record them in his transcription. In fact, except for the last steps of analysis and transcription, this is how we learn the sounds of our first language—by matching the results of our articulations with the sounds we hear.

As for perception, we have only a vague terminology for sound impressions, e.g., soft, hard, metallic, smooth, etc., which is useless for scientific purposes. Moreover, our judgments of sound similarity correspond to articulation anyway. Thus, other things being held constant, lip sounds are more similar to each other than those produced by articulating against the hard palate, etc. There is, however, one category of sound distinctions in which we resort to acoustic impression. This is the property of relative pitch.

Voiced sounds are produced by setting the vocal chords in motion so that they vibrate at a certain fundamental frequency. The same principle is involved in a reed instrument in music. Our impression of higher or lower pitch depends on the frequency of those vibrations—the faster the vibrations, the higher the pitch. These in turn depend on the degree of tension of the vocal chords and the force of the air flow through them. However, whereas we can make reliable judgments regarding higher and lower pitch based on acoustic impression, we cannot even become aware of the degree of tension of our vocal chords or the force of the air flow through them.

The third approach, the acoustic analysis of the sound wave itself, is accomplished by instrumental means. The most important of these is a machine known as the "sound spectrograph," which provides a visual display of the frequency spectrum of specimens of speech. This machine first became generally available after World War II, and research by means of it and other laboratory devices have made fundamental contributions to our knowledge of speech production and perception. We have learned for example that the brain is a kind of analyzer which gives us the impression of speech as a succession of discrete sounds each of which has constant characteristics in all its environments. For example, a k seems the same to us no matter what vowel it is followed by. But acoustic analysis shows that a k has no invariable single cue which distinguishes it from other sounds. This field, however, is so technical that we will not discuss it here.

Let's turn instead to articulation, particularly to the general principles of phonetic classification that underlie the analysis of the phonological structure of specific languages.

To understand these principles, however, we must first give an elementary description of the physical apparatus of speech production.[2] Speech sounds are normally produced by various modifications of the column of outgoing air produced by the lungs whose actions may be likened to that of a pump. This air first passes through the larynx or voice box whose most important structure is the glottis, which contains the vocal chords, more accurately called the "vocal folds." These folds, which have considerable elasticity, are capable of a number of adjustments. The two most important of these are that they are held far enough apart so that the air flows fully up and through them, or they are held so close together that the air coming through can set them into regular vibrations, in the course of which they open and close at a particular rate. The first adjustment leads to unvoiced sounds and the second to voiced sounds.

All the other modifications occur above the glottis and involve three anatomical structures. One of these is the velum, or soft palate. During most speech sounds it is raised, closing the nasal passage, so that air will come out only through the mouth and not the nose. If, however, it is not raised the air will pass through the nasal cavity and come out of the nose. This is the basis of the distinction between nonnasal and nasal sounds.

For example, in producing the *m* sound, the velum is low so that the air will come out of the nose. Since in this case the lips are also closed, the air in the mouth cavity behind the lips can only come out of the nose. In nasalized vowels, such as those found in French, although some air will escape through the mouth since for a vowel sound the oral cavity is not shut, because the velum is lowered, air will also come out of the nose to produce the nasal quality.

[2] For the articulation of English consonants, see Appendix B.

The second of the three chief speech organs above the glottis is the tongue, which is capable of producing numerous distinct articulations and is the main factor in generating the great variety of human speech sounds that we find. In fact, the basic distinction between vowels and consonants can be expressed in terms of the position of the tongue. For consonants, the tongue is raised sufficiently to make contact in some area with the roof of the mouth, thus producing various kinds of obstructions. For vowels, the tongue may be raised but not enough for the kind of obstruction required for consonants.

Tongue consonants involve three factors: the part of the tongue that makes the obstruction, the place in the mouth where the obstruction is made, and the manner in which the obstruction is made and released. Sounds are made by the tip of the tongue, the front immediately behind the tip, the middle of the tongue, and the back of the tongue. The place of articulation is partly dependent on the first factor. The tip of the tongue will naturally tend to make contact with forward parts of the mouth, e.g., the upper teeth or the gum ridge. However humans can turn the tip quite far back. Hence in this as in other sounds made by the tongue we must know both the part of the tongue involved and the place where the obstruction occurs, i.e., the place of articulation.

Manner involves both the type of obstruction and the type of release. For example, if the closure is complete and the release sudden, we have a stop consonant (e.g., *p, t, k*). If the obstruction is not complete but is only in the center of the tongue, allowing air to escape on one or both sides of the mouth, the sound is a lateral, as for example the *l* sound of English and many other languages. Another possibility is that the tongue is very close to the roof of the mouth at some point without making a complete obstruction, so that the air comes through a narrow aperture producing a noisy sound called a "fricative." In English *s* and *th* are among the fricatives. A third possibility combines the characteristics of stops and fricatives. There is first a closure as with a stop, but the release is gradual, producing a kind of friction sound similar to that of a fricative. Such a sound is called an "affricate." An example is the *ch* sound of English (as in "church"), the initial part involving an obstruction as for the *t* sound and the final part a fricative very similar to the English *sh* sound.

The combination of these different tongue positions and the various manners of closures and release allows the production of a very large number of distinct sounds. However, the possibilities are even more numerous than indicated above. The tongue is so flexible that different parts can carry out different articulations simultaneously. An example of such coarticulations are the palatalized consonants found, for example, in Russian. While some other part of the tongue is producing an obstruction elsewhere, the middle of the tongue may closely approach the back part of the hard palate producing a kind of simultaneous *y* consonantal sound known as palatalization.

For vowel sounds, we distinguish two fundamental factors. The first is a back-forward dimension based on which part of the tongue is raised. Although we are dealing with a continuum, we can make three distinctions—front, central, or back. In English the vowel of *bet* is a front vowel, the vowel of *cut* is a back vowel, while the unaccented vowel *e* in *open* is a central vowel.

The other factor is vowel height, which is determined by how high the tongue is raised. It is not difficult to distinguish at least three degrees of height—low, mid, and high—but again we are dealing with a continuum. In English the vowels of *hat, set,* and *pit* all involve the front of the tongue and are low, mid, and high respectively.

The final main articulator is the lips. The lips can, like the tongue, produce consonantal obstructions of various types. If both are involved the sound is classified as "bilabial." Thus, in English, *p* and *b* are bilabial stops, unvoiced and voiced respectively. The lower lip can likewise make contact with the upper teeth to produce a "labiodental" sound as in English *f* (unvoiced) and *v* (voiced). In addition, the lips play an important role in the production of vowels. By varying the shape of the opening of the mouth cavity from the extremes of rounding to spreading, they significantly modify the nature of the sound wave and, accordingly, the acoustic impression. In English the vowel of *boot* involves vigorous lip rounding, while that of *cat* involves neither rounding nor spreading. Such variation of the lip aperture, particularly rounding, also accompanies consonantal sounds, which are then said to be "labialized." Thus many languages have a unit sound found by a stop articulation of the back of the tongue against the soft palate (e.g., *k* if unvoiced) produced with simultaneous lip rounding [w]. It is thus something like but not identical to the initial sequence [kw], spelled *qu* in English words such as *quick*. In English we have both articulations but they are not simultaneous.

So far, we have been talking about sounds as if they were static. This is because each sound is defined by a set of specifications for the positions of the speech organs. But real speech consists of successions of sounds. Thus the word *cat* [k 'æ t=] would be described phonetically as a succession of three static positions, called "segments," i.e., an unvoiced aspirated velar stop [k'], followed by a front-low-unrounded vowel [æ], followed by an unvoiced unreleased alveolar (i.e., articulation against the upper front teeth ridge) stop. But in the actual speech chain we must have, physically speaking, transitional movements between these positions. Thus, to get from the [k] of *cat* to the following vowel, the tongue must move from a position where its back part is up against the soft palate for the [k] to a position where the front part is raised to enunciate the front vowel [æ]. The actual speech chain thus involves a series of movements. One of the striking results of acoustic research and x-ray photography for articulation is to show that these transitions are not merely short noiseless intervals; real speech involves constant movement in which the acoustic nature of the transitions are important and even dominant perceptual cues used in identifying the sequences of speech sounds. However, this need not destroy the value of an analysis in terms of successive segments if the transitions are predictable, which they are.

There are other aspects of speech which require us to conceive of speech in terms of sequences of segments. An example is duration. Many languages have two sets of vowel sounds, one short and the other long, based on the length of time it takes to articulate the vowel. However, this property of a particular vowel segment, unlike the tongue position which can be specified in isolation, is by its very nature relative. Often the long vowels in languages with this contrast last approximately twice as long as the short. Another example is pitch. What is significant in language is the relative pitch of successive voiced sounds. For example, many languages in various parts of the world such as Africa and Southeast Asia employ pitch differences to distinguish words of entirely different meanings. One common type involves the rule that the pitch of every syllable must be either high, middle, or low. What counts is the relative pitch of syllables when compared to each other in the speech chain. Thus the low pitch in a woman's speech might actually be higher than the high pitch of a man's speech.

In languages like English another relational feature is accent, which is the greater prominence of a syllable due to a combination of duration, loudness, and rapid pitch change. For example, in the word *capital,* the first syllable has a stress which depends on these factors. It is relational in that the first syllable is stronger compared to the other two.

In the preceding discussion we used the word "syllable." A syllable also is a basic unit which cannot be identified in isolation because it rests on the successive opening and closing of the vocal tract. The center of a syllable is a segment which is more open than that which precedes or follows it. It is normally a vowel because the vowel involves the most unobstructed opening of the vocal tract. The number of syllables is the number of such centers. The center may on occasion be a consonant which is more open than the preceding and following consonants. An example is *l,* which is a relatively open consonant since the only closure is the contact between the central part of the tongue and the roof of the mouth. Thus the air may escape on either or both sides of the tongue, producing a relatively open and sonorous air chamber, which is responsible for its vowellike quality. For example, the word *cattle* has two syllables and for most speakers the second consists entirely of the consonant *l* which is more open than the preceding consonant *t.* Here the *l* functions as the center of a syllable just as a vowel does.

These relational sounds are often called "prosodic," in contrast to the segmental, or static, positional sounds discussed earlier.

Any sound can be described by a finite and, in fact, small number of specifications, which are called "features." Why is this? Well, the articulations of speech consist of a number of different movements of different organs or parts of organs (e.g., the tip of the tongue) which are independent of each other. Each one of these in turn has a number of possibilities which mutually exclude each other. For example, what the glottis does is independent of what the tongue or lips do. The vocal folds may vibrate whether the lips are closed or not. On the other hand, the glottis cannot be open and not vibrate and be closed and vibrate at the same time. A glottal feature therefore has *at least* two values: voicing and voicelessness. Similarly, for any sound we may have the feature of bilabiality which takes one value if the lips are closed and another if they are open. We usually symbolize these alternatives with + and − respectively. For example, if a particular sound in a language is articulated with an obstruction at the lips it is + *bilabial* (i.e., [p]), if not, it is − *bilabial* (i.e., [k]). Looked at this way, any specific sound of a language can be phonetically specified by a bundle of values of such features.

Not all of the possible values of all features are found in any single language. Every language uses a limited number. When a particular value of a feature occurs in one sound in a language, it is likely to occur in a number of others. For example, in English, voicing occurs in a whole series of consonants such as *b, d, g, v, j, z,* etc., which thus constitutes a class. There are languages, however, like Chinese, which, outside of nasals and liquid sounds like *r* and *l,* lack voiced consonants. Thus the sounds of a language can be described in terms of the combinations of a very limited number of recurrent features.

So far we have only considered the classifications of sounds on the phonetic level. Hence, in terms of our example at the beginning of the chapter in regard to aspiration in English and Hindi, both languages would be said to have the feature value of aspiration since both have aspirated consonants. However, we saw that aspiration functions differently in the two languages. In English, the distinction between the non-aspirate and aspirated forms of *t* could never distinguish between two different words, whereas in Hindi it would.

In English this is a systematic aspect of the sound system. The other unvoiced stops, *p* and *k*, likewise have aspirated forms which, just as in the case of *t*, do not distinguish one word from another. Similarly in Hindi, just as there is a significant contrast between /t/ and /t'/ so there are corresponding contrasts between /p/ and /p'/, /k/ and /k'/ and other pairs. While we can still talk of features, we can now say that in Hindi aspiration is a "distinctive feature" because its presence or absence distinguishes different words. In English, however, aspiration is present as a *phonetic* feature but, unlike Hindi, it is a nondistinctive feature in the *phonological* system of the language.

Another somewhat different type of example in English is voicing in regard to nasals. Nasal consonants such as *m* and *n* in English are generally pronounced with vibration of the vocal chords. Hence they have voicing as a phonetic feature. However, since this feature is predictable in the case of nasals, we may say it is "redundant" or "nondistinctive" in this case. In other words, for English, from the nasality of a segment we can predict its voicing, hence voicing is nondistinctive. This is not true of all languages. For example, Irish has a contrast between voiced and unvoiced nasals.

In the above examples we identified a feature by choosing between presence or absence, e.g., presence or absence of nasality, presence or absence of aspiration. If we could define all features in this way, we might simply symbolize the presence of a particular feature by + and its absence by —, and where, as with voicing in English nasals, the value is predictable, it could be left blank.

For example, Figure 4 shows a portion of the consonantal system of Sanskrit, the classical literary language of India.

The phonemes are arranged here in a form frequently found in grammars. All phonemes in the same column have

	1	2	3	4	5
Ia	p	t	ṭ	c	k
Ib	p'	t'	ṭ'	c'	k'
IIa	b	d	ḍ	j	g
IIb	b'	d'	ḍ'	j'	g'
III	m	n	ṇ	ñ	ṅ

Figure 4.

the same point of articulation. These are numbered 1 to 5, from the front to the back of the mouth and are bilabial (lips), apical (tongue tip), retroflex (tongue tip turned back), palatal (articulated against the hard palate), and velar (against the soft palate).

All sounds in rows Ia and Ib are unvoiced nonnasal stops; in IIa and b, all are voiced nonnasal stops; and in III, all are nasal. Those in Ia and IIa are unaspirated and those in Ib and IIb are aspirated. Evidently any of the phonemes can be distinguished from all of the others by a small number of feature specifications. For example p would be +bilabial, −voice, −aspiration, −nasal, +stop.

The Sanskrit example is perhaps somewhat unrepresentative, in that not every sound system is quite so tightly organized. Not all possible combinations of features will occur in other systems, so there will be some gaps in them. Still, they can always be described as resulting from the simultaneous occurrence of a very small number of features. In fact, all the thousands of systems of the world's languages can be generated from a very limited common pool of such features, just as the combination of a limited number of genes produces all the variations of human heredity. Not one of the phonetic features found in Sanskrit is unique to it. It has even been proposed that there are only twelve such principles of contrast, selections from which would be sufficient to specify all the sound systems of the world; others suggest a larger number, but in any case they would not be more than thirty. The individual phonemes produced by combining these are also found to vary within narrow limits from language to language. The smallest number is about fifteen, found in some Polynesian languages, while the greatest number are about sixty, as in some Caucasian languages. For most languages, the range is from thirty to fifty.

Chapter 4

GRAMMATICAL THEORY

We have seen that every language has a coherently organized set of sound units called "phonemes."

But every language also has a syntagmatic system for its words; in English, for example, a word may only begin with certain phonemes which can then only occur in a certain order.

However, in any language there will be numerous sequences of sounds which, while they do not violate any phonological rules, nevertheless do not occur. For example, there is no rule that would prevent us from having a word *snab /snæb/. The initial sequence *sn* conforms to the rules of English. Moreover, *sn* may be followed by the vowel /æ/ as in *snack* /snæk/, and /æ/ may be followed by /b/ in word final position as in the word *nab* /næb/.

But, we might argue, *snack* and *nab* each *mean* something, whereas *snab* is not a meaningful sequence in English. And we'd be right. Examples of this sort are on a "higher" level than phonological ones, since they involve the distinction between meaningless and meaningful combinations of the elements isolated on the phonological level.

This higher level is that of grammar. Its tasks are far more complex than specifying which possible sequences are meaningful. For example, not just any random sequence of words that conveys a distinct meaning is an acceptable grammatical sentence. The problem of grammatical theory, then, is to delineate the rules governing the formation of acceptable sequences of meaningful elements.

The most elementary functional unit on the grammatical level is not necessarily the word. Words such as *now, here,* and *with* cannot be divided into smaller parts, each with its own meaning. But more complex words, such as *blackbird, singer,* and *advertisement* can be divided into meaningful shorter sequences. Moreover, such sequences are subject to rules and the rules must belong to grammar and not phonology. For example, the word *sing-er* is divisible into two parts, one of which signifies the act of singing and the other, *-er,* the agent. In English numerous nouns are derived from verbs in this way and the *-er* is said to be a "suffix" since its position is fixed in that it always follows the verb root. Grammar then cannot consist only of rules that govern the way words are combined with each other, but also must include rules that specify how more elementary units are combined to form the words themselves. Linguists call these more elementary units "morphemes."

Assuming that the word is a valid unit at some level of analysis, grammar then falls quite naturally into two subdivisions. One has to do with the internal structure of words and is traditionally called "morphology." The other has to do with the way in which words themselves combine to form higher structural units such as phrases, clauses, and sentences. We call the latter "syntax."

Morphology really covers two different topics, word formation and inflection, but it is most often used for inflection.

To grasp the difference between word formation and inflection, let us consider a complex word such as *farmers.* We can divide it into three separate morphemes, or minimal meaning units: *farm-, -er-,* and *-s.* These elements are different. The first one, *farm-,* has the most concrete meaning. The meaning of *-er* is more abstract, that of agent or "one who does." Finally, the *-s* of the plural is the most abstract of all. The grammatical functions of these elements also differ. The *-er* is a "derivational morpheme." It can never occur in isolation and its function is to form more complex words from roots like *farm-.* (The other important method of deriving more complex words is compounding, in which two roots are put together to form a new word, for example, *gunslinger* or *strawberry*.)

The function of the final *-s* of *farmer-s* is quite different from the derivational function of *-er*. It does not form a new word with a different dictionary meaning, but expresses a category of the complex *farm-er*, namely plurality.

Morphemes like the *-s* plural are generally called "inflectional." Characteristically, they involve a choice among a very small number of alternatives of highly abstract meaning—e.g., plural as against singular in the present instance—and have syntactic relations to other words in the sentence. For example, the presence of the plural *-s* in *farmers* makes us choose *these* rather than *this* and *work* rather than *works* as in the sentence "This farmer works; these farmers work."

The example of *farm-er-s* shows that a complex word has an internal structure consisting of differentiated morphemes, in this case, root, derivational, and inflectional, respectively. This example illustrates two additional properties of word structure. The first is that the order is fixed. Just as in phonology where only certain consonant sequences may occur and only in a certain order, so in morphology not only is the order of morphemes fixed within a particular word—i.e., one cannot say **farm-s-er* or **s-er-farm*—but this order is indicative of the basic rule of order in English that inflectional elements such as number in the noun, comparison in the adjective, and tense in the verb are always final, while derivational elements like *-er-* follow the root and precede the inflection. Only one additional fact is necessary to mention: there are a small number of derivational elements which may precede the root and thus occupy the initial position in the word, for example, the *re-* of verbs like *reread, reload*, etc.

The second is that when more than two elements are in a construction as in the case of *farm-er-s*, there is a certain hierarchy in the way they are put together. For example, *-s* forms the plural of *farm-er* just as it forms the plural of *boy*, even though *boy*, unlike *farmer*, is not divisible into parts. We can symbolize this hierarchy with parentheses, as follows: (*farm-er*)-*s*. This means that the *-er-* goes more closely with *farm-* than with *-s*. The principle we use here is that of "immediate constituents." Thus, the immediate constituents of *farm-er-s* are *farm-er* and *-s*. The method of immediate constituents is basic to grammatical analysis and works on all levels. In a long sentence there might easily be as many as fifty morphemes. Unless some elements were more closely related to form subordinate units, there would be no place to begin to break down and analyze such a complex structure.

An example of a fairly intricate structure on the syntactic level is the modal auxiliary phrase in English. Modal auxiliaries include verbs such as *can, may, should,* etc.

One of the simplest of modal auxiliary phrases consists of modal auxiliaries followed by the simple infinitive of the main verb, that is, the form obtained by omitting *to* in such examples as *to go, to eat, to be.* This two-member structure can be diagrammed according to the now familiar scheme in which the sequential relations are shown horizontally and the paradigmatic class membership relations vertically, as in Figure 5.

1	2
can	be
could	have
may	eat
might	go
shall	sing
should	come
will	see
would	etc.

Figure 5.

An important difference between class 1 and class 2 is expressed by the etc. Class 1 has a very limited inventory and new members can be added only by very complex historical changes over a considerable period of time. It is thus very much like the inflectional morphemes, e.g., those for singular and plural. Such classes are called "closed" and usually have a highly abstract meaning. Class 2 is called "open." Not only is the number of members vast, including all the thousands of main verbs of English, but it can also be added to fairly easily by grammatical innovation. Thus, recently *parent* and *impact,* in addition to their usual and older usage as nouns, have come to be used as verbs, e.g., in a recently published book entitled *How to Parent.* The meanings here are also generally concrete compared to those of class 1, e.g., *eat, drink, walk, sleep.*

The verbs of class 1 come in pairs—*can/could; may/might; shall/should; will/would.* Historically, the second members of each pair are past tenses of the first members. Further, although the first members are like present tenses as opposed to past tenses, they do not have *-s* in the third person singular. Thus, one cannot say **he cans go.* Regarding the auxiliaries *shall* and *will,* traditional grammar, based on Latin, singles them out as forming a future tense in which capacity they participate in a three-way distinction of past, present, and future. From the present structural analysis we see that *shall* and *will* belong with the other modal auxiliaries.

Among the verbs in column 2, are two, *be* and *have,* which possess a special status. They function both as main verbs, as in Figure 5, and as auxiliaries in their own right. One of these, *be,* may be followed by the present active participle ending in *-ing* to indicate "progressive," or "continuous action," e.g., *they are going.* It may also be used with the past participle, which in many verbs ends in *-ed* and has a passive meaning, e.g., *they are added.* The verb *have* as an auxiliary is followed by the same past participle to indicate completed action, e.g., *they have added.*

As modal auxiliaries, they act as second auxiliaries, themselves governed by modals, and in turn governing a main verb. This pattern is shown below in Figure 6.

1	2	3
may	be	eating
might	be	eaten
can	have	eaten
could	be	eating
etc.	etc.	etc.

Figure 6.

The complexities become even greater when we consider negative and interrogative forms, which involve regular changes in the order of the elements, e.g., *can they have been eaten? they can't have been eaten.* In spite of these apparent intricacies, however, there are certain basically simple rules. The order in each construction is fixed. The modals always take the simple infinitive, *be* takes the present or past participle to mean progressive and passive respectively, and *have* takes the past participle to indicate completed action.

A significant characteristic of the syntactic construction is that it may sometimes be indefinitely expanded. For example, in the noun phrases, adjectives may be added without limit. Although every phrase must be finite in length, there is a mechanism by which it can always be made longer. This is much like what is meant by infinity in mathematics: the natural numbers constitute an infinite set because given any number, I can always name the next higher number. So with a sentence or any syntactic construction, I can always add another clause beginning "and." Hence the number of possible noun phrases or sentences is infinite although each individual instance must of course be finite in length.

This does not occur on the morphological level. Another way of stating this is to note that there is such a thing as the longest word in English. It is sometimes said to be "antidis-establishmentarianism." If this is so, all the words can be ordered by length and alphabetically within the group of any particular length. They can then be counted and are finite in number. This is why a dictionary of finite length is always possible. On the other hand, there is no such thing as the longest possible sentence in English. We can always make it longer. This means that they can never be merely listed and a grammar on the syntactic level tells us the methods by which, from the finite resources of the dictionary, this theoretically infinite number of sentences can be formed.

In summary, linguistic structures on levels as different as the phonological, morphological, and syntactic show a number of fundamentally similar traits in their organization, such as fixed order of elements, differentiated classes, and hierarchical dependency relations. An essential contribution of twentieth-century structuralism was to discover, document, and analyze such basic traits of structure.

Another basic achievement of the structuralist approach is the development of a methodology through which a scientific observer can to a considerable extent overcome the biases from his own linguistic background, and describe each language in terms of its own significant categories and not on the basis of those derived from the observer's language. Regarding this we will consider phonology and grammar separately.

When we hear the sounds of a foreign language, we naturally perceive them in terms of those of our own language. Where phonetic distinctions exist that are not part of our linguistic background, we will often fail to hear them as different; even if we do recognize them as somehow different, we cannot, without training, recognize exactly what these differences are. The first step, taken in the nineteenth century, was to analyze speech sounds in terms of mainly articulatory features and to map all these possibilities and provide a method of transcription in order to record them. A well-trained observer could then accurately record the sounds of a foreign language even when they differed from his own. When instrumental phonetics began to develop towards the end of the nineteenth century, it seemed to many that the goal, which was merely to record sounds accurately, could be attained by the use of laboratory methods.

However, it turned out that a physical acoustic record was, in a sense, too accurate and did not provide useful categories for the analysis of sounds as actually used in languages. Even the same vowel produced by the same person in the same word on different occasions produced a different acoustic record. As the ancient philosopher Heraclitus noted, "The same man never crosses the same river." Nor could constant characteristics be found in the acoustic record so that, by disregarding certain variations, it would be possible to correlate the physical wave phenomena with the speaker's and linguist's own impressions as to what was the same sound.

Hence the realization began to grow that it was not sufficient merely to record accurately what was either audibly different to the trained ear or visibly different in the instrumental phonetic record. Even sounds which were phonetically the same to the qualified observer were not really the same to speakers of different languages, because they were organized differently and played a different role in their systems. In other words, it was not merely necessary to say when sounds were different physically but how, for example, a contrast of two sounds in one language might function to distinguish different words while the same two sounds, while present in another language, might never be used for such a purpose. In the latter case, speakers are generally unaware of or even unable to perceive the difference between the sounds. Structuralist phonology thus makes it possible to show the functioning units of each language in terms of its own organization.

In the area of grammar, parallel problems existed in the nineteenth century. Traditional grammar in the West is based on the Roman grammarians who applied the methods first developed by the Greeks to their own language. It was possible to apply the categories worked out by the Greek grammarians to Latin because the languages were historically related and very similar in over-all structure. For example, both languages had case, number, and gender in the noun, and the adjective agreed with the noun in these three categories. The verbs of both Greek and Latin were inflected for person and number of the subject and for tense, mood, and voice. While there were minor differences, the two languages often coincided even in details such as the existence of a particular case, the dative, to signify the indirect object. To begin with, people tried to apply this model to modern European languages in a quite literal way.

For example, in Latin each noun had six different case forms expressed by different endings. Each case had a series of syntactic uses, i.e., each was used to indicate different kinds of relations between the noun and other words in the sentence. Thus, if *Marcus* was the subject of a verb it took the nominative form: *Marcus vēnit* 'Marcus comes', but if *Marcus* was the object, it took the accusative form: *interfēcit Marcum* 'He killed Marcus'. But in English, except for the possessive *'s*, no case change is ever made in the form of the noun. The relations are expressed by other means; in older grammars of English, for example, one might find the following:

Noun Declension

Nominative	man
Genitive	of the man
Dative	to the man
Accusative	man
Ablative	from the man
Vocative	O man!

Figure 7.

In such instances a set of cases based on another language (in this case, Latin) has been imposed. In English *man* does not change. Moreover, if *from the man* is an ablative (literally, in Latin, "carry away"), then why not *with the man* as a "comitative case," *behind the man* as a "posterior case," and so on indefinitely?

The attempt to write grammars of languages like the American Indian ones, which differ far more from Latin than English does, led to even more drastic questioning of the traditional scheme based on Greek and Latin.

The earlier basic assumption had been that all languages have the same categories. Therefore those of the classical languages were thought as good as any others for describing any language whatsoever. This meant that the grammatical approach would be through meaning. In asking, for example, what the genitive case was in some exotic language, the grammarian answered the question by a translation equivalent, just as in the example of English above. How one translated *of the man* in the language under study was investigated to discover how the genitive case was expressed.

The essence of the structuralist alternative to this method was to turn to form instead of meaning. A category such as tense was a grammatically significant one in a language if it was expressed by a set of meaningful elements like morphemes or words. These classes, in turn, were determined functionally. Two or more items belong to a class if one can be used in place of the other and we still get a grammatically possible utterance. On this basis, one can question the validity of even the most fundamental aspects of the traditional scheme. Once we decide not to use meaning equivalence as the basis for distinguishing categories, we can ask questions more fundamental than the existence or non-existence of specific cases like the nominative or dative.

Traditional grammar was based on the notion that all the words of the language could be divided into a relatively small number of classes called parts of speech—nouns, verbs, adjectives, adverbs, etc. Whether all languages had these parts of speech became an open question for structuralists. In traditional grammar such parts of speech were defined quite loosely, sometimes by semantic criteria, sometimes by formal criteria, and often enough by some combination of the two. Thus a noun was defined formally in classical grammar as a class of words that was inflected for number, case, and gender and/or semantically as the "name of a person, place, or thing," or the like.

Structuralists generally rejected semantic criteria for defining functional linguistic categories. But formal criteria with which they were willing to operate were not universally applicable. In many languages the categories of case, number, and gender were lacking. In fact, there were some languages, like Chinese, which lacked all three of these. How, then, could such languages be said to have nouns?

But if every language has its own system of word classes (parts of speech) or, more generally, linguistic categories such as tense, mood, and case, and there is no structural comparability among them, linguistics becomes incapable of arriving at conclusions about language in general, which surely should be its aim.

This is one of the basic weaknesses of the structural approach to language, and recent work in the area of language universals both from within and independently of recent transformational theory have sought to resolve this question.

The discussion of this topic will be the central theme of the last chapter of the present work.

The other basic weakness of structuralism was that while the scheme of structuralist analysis illustrated in Chapters 2 and 3 and the earlier sections of this present chapter provided important insights into the systematic nature of language, it was found to be defective as a general model for describing individual languages.

As an answer to these inadequacies, the last twenty-five years or so has seen the rise of a quite different theory of grammar, known as the "generative transformational theory," initiated by Noam Chomsky. This approach uses a quasi-mathematical symbolism and is so complex that it can hardly be discussed in any detail in a work of this scope.

Yet we can indicate a few of the grammatical phenomena which could not be easily or naturally handled within the framework of American structuralism. One of these had to do with systematic relationships between sets of sentences where each of the sentence types was significantly different in respect to the positional classes and their sequences as they would be described by structuralist theory. An example of this is the active and passive. A pair of sentences such as "The man ate the steak" and "The steak was eaten by the man" differ in that some of the words in the second sentence belong to a paradigmatic class not found in the first and that even when the same classes are found, their order in the sentence is partly different. To a structuralist, therefore, they were distinct constructions.

However, this is not an isolated pair of sentences. There are innumerable others related in the same way. The systematic rules by which such pairs of sentences are related would seem to belong to the grammar of the language and to be part of the knowledge of speakers who use it. Such systematic relationships between large classes of sentences are known as transformational relationships and occur in all languages.

It becomes an explicit goal of grammatical theory to generalize as far as possible. Thus, if we give a rule transforming an active to a passive, it must be highly general in form, making clear the characteristics of the entire class of active sentences to which the passive transformation applies and the recurrent methods by which the change is carried out. We must also give the order in which transformations should be applied. For example, there is a question transformation by which we derive the structure of sentences like "Did the cat eat the mouse?" from the sentence "The cat ate the mouse." Such question transformations also apply to the passive counterpart of "The cat ate the mouse" ("Was the mouse eaten by the cat?"). To state the rule for the question transformation as generally as possible, it will be necessary first to allow for the derivation of passives and then to apply the question transformation to either type, active or passive.

Hence transformational grammar involves a series of operations on highly abstract general symbols. This underlying structure, sometimes called the "deep structure," sets out the basic grammatical and semantic relationships. It is only at a later stage that specific vocabulary items are substituted for the general symbols. Once this form has been subject to any transformation rules, like the ones illustrated above for the question, the outcome is the actual sentence, or "surface structure."

Another large group of phenomena which can be treated by similar transformational methods are certain types of ambiguous sentences. For example, "They are flying planes" has two different semantic interpretations. In one it is parallel, for example, to "They are rabbits" and in the other to "They are eating bananas." But in an analysis by grammatical classes and their sequences, it is argued, they would be identical. The solution within the transformational framework is to derive this sentence from two underlying, or deep, structures of different kinds indicated by different symbols.

This approach has undergone very elaborate developments in a brief period of time. And it has given rise to difficulties. Alternative deep-structure analyses are often possible and espoused by different linguists, and no generally accepted principles have been developed to decide such cases. In recent years even more drastically different alternative forms of transformational theory have appeared. Nevertheless, just like structuralism before it, the transformational approach has provided new insights and made possible real progress in our understanding of linguistic phenomena.

Chapter 5

SEMANTIC THEORY

The scientific study of meaning is called "semantics." To most people, meaning is the most interesting aspect of language. After all, the basic purpose of language is to communicate, and the ultimate purpose of voice sounds and grammatical rules is the construction of meaningful utterances.

Yet semantics is the most controversial and the least scientifically developed area of linguistics. Remember that structuralists approached language through form rather than meaning and were distrustful of the traditional attempt to define universal grammatical categories through meaning. For one thing, they felt that, whereas sounds and grammatical sequences of sounds seemed to be directly and empirically observable, meanings were far more abstract and difficult to grasp. Furthermore, meanings referred to things outside of language itself and required, in a sense, a total knowledge of the external world, which was for any person unattainable. If, for example, we want to understand the meaning of "star," we should go to the astronomer, not the linguist in his capacity as lexicographer or dictionary maker. Similarly, we should go to the psychologist to understand the meaning of "envy," and so on.

Recently, however, linguists have turned more and more to the serious study of the semantic side of language. In doing so, they have been largely preceded by philosophers, particularly logicians, since logic demands attention to the linguistic aspects of meaning. Further, language itself has been a subject of philosophical speculation even from the time of the ancient Greeks, and most of this interest has been in semantics.

A good place to begin is with the word "meaning" itself. If semantics is the study of meaning, what does "meaning" itself mean? The word "meaning" has a number of distinct meanings of the sort that large dictionaries number and list separately. Of the meanings relevant to linguistics, there are at least two of major importance which divide semantics rather clearly into two distinct though interrelated subfields. These two are (1) the meaning of a single lexical item, such as the word "horse" and (2) the meaning of a sentence, such as "There is a large house on the corner."

Since the number of words is finite, it is possible to list them, which is exactly what is done in a dictionary. But the number of possible sentences is infinite. The rules of grammar specify the ways in which words can be combined into sentences. Such grammatical synthesis is paralleled by a semantic synthesis, in which what are grammatical units at various levels are each meaningful and contribute to the meaning of the sentence as a whole. For example, in the above sentence, "There is a large house on the corner," just as *house on* is not a grammatical constituent, so also it has no meaning; but the prepositional phrase *on the corner* is a grammatically valid part of the sentence and it somehow does seem "meaningful" when taken in isolation.

Given the infinity of grammatically possible sentences, the meanings of sentences cannot be treated as a list as the meanings of vocabulary items are. Rather, there must be certain semantic interpretation rules at various levels leading up to the interpretation of the sentence as a whole.

On the basis of this distinction between the meaning of vocabulary items and the meaning of syntactic constructions in a sentence, the study of semantics is divided into what are called "lexical semantics" and "sentence interpretation semantics."

Traditionally, the results of lexical semantic research in a particular language is embodied in a dictionary. Since dictionaries are intended for practical use, the items are ordered alphabetically so that we can locate them quickly. From a theoretical point of view this order is entirely arbitrary. For instance, we could have ordered our dictionaries by parts of speech instead. However, out of practical necessity we adopt a generally agreed upon ordering, however arbitrary in principle. In any case, we are left with the scientific question of whether or not the lexical items of a language possess some kind of over-all structure, as is true with phonology and grammar. If so, what is this structure like and how can it be investigated?

Traditional lexicography in addition to listing all vocabulary items of a language, provides each one with one or more definitions. This is a further indication of the fundamental difference between lexical and sentence interpretation semantics. We define a word but not a sentence. The next question, then, concerns the nature and types of definitions and the criteria for their adequacy. This question is clearly connected with the one mentioned above, namely, the over-all structure of vocabulary. Presumably we do not compare words as such but various more fundamental features that go into their definition. A further question then concerns what constitutes a unit entry. To say that a dictionary lists all the words of a language is not adequate and in fact does not conform with actual practice of dictionary makers. For example, *sing* and *sang* are in a sense different words, but they are not entered separately in dictionaries. If we say a dictionary contains all the words of a language, we must first make clear what we mean by a word for purposes of dictionary making.

There are, then, three basic questions in lexicographical semantics: the over-all structure of vocabulary, the nature and requirements of definition, and the exact nature of a basic unit entry. All three of these are complex problems, and they are listed here in what may be plausibly viewed as the order of decreasing complexity. We shall consider the simplest first.

The first question, then, involves the unit of lexical semantics. In lexicography it makes sense to start with the actual practice of lexicographers since it is they who, with a minimum of over-all theory, actually compile the dictionaries.

The basic unit of the lexicographer is the main entry, that is, a word of the language under which one or more separate meanings are given, along with additional information such as its historical origin. In addition, dictionaries list whole phrases whose meaning is not obvious from that of the individual words which compose them. There are also minor entries like the irregular tense forms of verbs. Under *took* we might find the notation that it is past of *take,* but we are referred to the latter as a main entry for fuller information. That the main entry should be a word is not to be taken entirely for granted.

Structuralists consider that since a word is often analyzable into parts, the smallest unit with a meaning is a morpheme. Accordingly, certain linguists using this approach have considered a dictionary to be a list of morphemes with their meanings, and have occasionally compiled such dictionaries, usually for "exotic" languages. Such a dictionary is of value to students of historical comparative linguistics since the reduction of words to their root elements facilitates comparison with related languages. However, since the rules of combination and modification of the morpheme for making up words are often very complicated, only a person who already has an explicit knowledge of the grammar of the language can use it. Therefore, even native speakers have trouble using this kind of dictionary if they are not themselves linguists. The average person thinks in terms of words in his own language, which are coherent sequences of sound and are pronounceable in isolation.

There is a further problem in word derivation where formatives are highly irregular and idiosyncratic. A morpheme dictionary of English with an entry *-ity* meaning *state, condition, quality,* or *degree* used to form abstract nouns from adjectives, should also list all of the stems with which it can combine since these cannot be stated by any simple rule. For example, given *rigid-ity* one might also expect **pliant-ity*.

Where would we find such information in an over-all description of English? The grammar of English is concerned with rules including recurrent formations. If an English grammar listed all the possibilities of occurrence with such terminations as *-ation, -ency,* etc., it would be endless.

This illustrates an essential point. Ideally, we might want a "complete" description of a language to contain a phonology, a grammar, and a dictionary. But then, how would we discriminate between the grammar and the dictionary? Well, a grammar contains everything that is reducible to rules while the dictionary contains whatever is not predictable by rules. The listing of meanings is central to a dictionary simply because it is the most important aspect of language not predictable by any over-all rules. I may know all the grammatical rules of German there are, but there is no rule that will tell me that the word for *table* is *Tisch.* Further, it won't tell me that *Tisch* is masculine grammatically. All German nouns are either masculine, feminine, or neuter in gender and this affects their inflection, the choice of correct forms for the article and adjectives used with it, and so on. Such choices are governed by rules that are found in grammars. But to know which rules to apply, I must first know that *Tisch* is masculine. And, in fact, German dictionaries do list the gender of each noun as part of the dictionary entry.

Thus dictionary makers are justified, theoretically as well as practically, in choosing the word as the unit for dictionary entries. However, although every dictionary's main entry is a word (with a few exceptions such as fixed phrases and abbreviations which are standardized in the orthography), not every word is a dictionary entry. Thus, in most dictionaries of English, one will not find such words as *presented,* *tables,* and *broader.* To find their meanings one will, of course, have to look under *present, table,* and *broad,* respectively.

So a dictionary entry is not a word as such. Each word stands for the whole family of inflected forms, if it has inflections, and is called a "paradigm." Thus, the verb *bite* is the main entry not only for *bite* but also for *bites, biting, bit,* and *bitten.* We can consider such a family of forms a kind of unit on a higher level, a set with the following members: (bite, bites, biting, bit, bitten). An uninflected word like *now,* is simply a limiting case in which a paradigm is a set with a single member.

In the above example, one member of the set, *bite,* has a privileged status in that it is the one to be selected as the actual entry. Further, it is always the same form that is selected—the singular in the noun, the positive as against the comparative and the superlative in the adjective, and the form used with *to* to form the infinitive in the verb.

Is the choice of these forms arbitrary or can it be justified by some principle? There does seem to be at least some intuitive basis for the particular selection. It would somehow be strange to look for *large* in a dictionary under *larger.* Yet the opposite is quite natural. Moreover, persons with little knowledge of grammar conform to these choices quite easily when learning to use a dictionary.

The priority of a particular grammatical form as the representative of the entire paradigm has a basis in linguistic theory. It involves an aspect of hierarchy that we have not considered up to now but which is central to contemporary theory and has wider ramifications.

The chosen grammatical form is generally called the "unmarked" form and the whole topic is known as "marking theory." Consider the singular and plural forms of the noun. The plural is, in the literal sense, "marked," as against the "unmarked" singular, in that it is usually expressed by the additional sound sequence spelled *-s* or *-es,* while the singular is indicated by the absence of such a mark. This is another characteristic of the unmarked form which indicates that it is more fundamental. For example, the singular of nouns occurs far more often than the plural (the ratio is about four to one). Moreover, such facts seem not to be confined to English. In most languages the plural is more complex in that it involves a mark of some kind and occurs less frequently. Also, the unmarked category as the more basic form tends to be more differentiated. For example, in a gender language like French or German it often happens that gender distinctions are made only in the singular and are merged in the plural. The term used by linguists for this phenomenon is "neutralization" and can be seen in French where in the singular a masculine noun takes the definite article *le* and a feminine noun *la* but in the plural this distinction is neutralized so that there is only one form, *les*, to cover both categories.

In summary, the dictionary entry is a word that functions as the representative of an entire set of inflected forms of the same lexeme. The word form generally chosen is the unmarked one. But what about homonyms, that is, words which sound alike and are spelled the same way but have a different meaning? Is *bank* in the meaning "bank of a river" a different item from *bank* in its meaning an institution in which one deposits money? Are they two different dictionary entries, say $bank_1$ and $bank_2$?

The concept of lexeme is often crucial to the solution of this problem. Certain questions can be answered, once we realize that we are dealing with different lexemes represented by the same "words" in the phonetic and graphic sense. For example, *bear* as a verb and *bear* as a noun are clearly separate items and therefore true homonyms. The first *bear* represents the verb set (to bear, bears, bearing, bore, born) and the second the noun set, (bear, bears). This follows naturally from their belonging to two differently inflected parts of speech.

But other cases cannot be decided this easily. *Bank* is a noun in both of the above meanings and has the same plural in either meaning. The mere existence of two distinguishable meanings does not necessarily mean that we should have two entries. In fact, most common words have a variety of meanings which are usually given as separate numbered items under a single dictionary entry. In such instances, the average speaker of the language does feel that he is dealing with the "same word" in spite of the different meanings because these meanings are somehow related aspects of the same word. For example *chair* in the meaning of an established and frequently endowed position at a university or again as a term for the presiding person at a meeting as in "the chair recognized so-and-so" are probably felt by most speakers of English to be the same word as *chair*, the well-known piece of furniture, and, indeed, dictionaries generally list all these meanings and still others as individual items under a common entry.

One solution, then, is an appeal to the feelings of speakers. But to test this systematically and objectively for an entire dictionary is obviously impractical in terms of time and money and has never been seriously considered. In practice, this criterion is carried out by the lexicographer himself on the grounds that he is also a speaker of the language and his judgment is at least as valid as anyone else's.

The other criterion often employed by dictionary makers is the history of the word in question. With this approach, homonyms could be defined as otherwise identical words which differ in meaning because in the past they were distinct words with different pronunciations as well. Their present resemblance results from changes through which they have coincided in pronunciation. Another possibility is that one was a distinct word borrowed from a foreign language which just happened to have the same sound as another word in the English language. In other words, a true homonym is a result of a kind of historical accident.

Take the verb *to blow*. In its meaning, largely confined to poetry, of *to bloom*, it derives from the Old English *blōwan*, whereas in the sense of air stirring or being stirred into motion it comes from Old English *blāwan*. Both of these are historically distinct from the noun *blow*, a forcible stroke, which descends from Middle English *blaw, blowe*.

On the other hand, the multiple meanings of what is psychologically viewed as a single word generally arises from the shifts of meaning of what was originally the same word. The basis for such shifts of meaning is often obvious, as for example, *chair* in the meaning of someone who presides at a meeting. Sometimes, however, historical and psychological factors can be in conflict. For example, some people, at least, think that *horn* in its meaning as a musical instrument is probably distinct from its meaning as the body part of an animal. But historically they are differentiated meanings of the same original word and the Oxford English Dictionary lists them under the same word.

We now come to what would generally be considered the central task of dictionaries, namely, to inform the reader of the meaning or meanings of an entry. This is commonly called "definition" and is a very wide subject. We will try to point to a few aspects of definition that concern linguists. First, except for the illustrations in some dictionaries, included, no doubt, on the principle that one picture is worth a thousand words, dictionaries define words by means of other words and therefore assume certain linguistic knowledge on the part of the reader. There are two different types of dictionary, the monolingual and bilingual. In a bilingual dictionary, e.g., in a Spanish-English dictionary, one word is explained by translation into another language, knowledge of which is assumed. Hence the tendency is to give a definition by single words in one language or by a set of synonymous words in another. Insofar as there is reasonable meaning identity between languages, and it does exist to a considerable extent, it is merely a matter of finding an equivalence. For example, for the Spanish word *cabeza*, one can give English *head*, without explaining in a phrase or sentence what *head* means in English. Of course, many cases are not that "simple." Since each language is likely to have a number of meanings for each word, it is important to point out that, e.g., *cabeza* does not equate with some of the meanings of English *head*, e.g., head of a school, which is *jefe* 'chief' in Spanish.

In a monolingual dictionary, we must explain the meaning of a word in the language itself. This is generally called "periphrasis" and raises many difficulties. For example, for a definition to serve its purpose, the reader must know the meanings of the words in the definition itself. Almost everyone has had the experience in using a dictionary of looking up a word, finding a word in the definition, not knowing its meaning, then looking up this word, and finding the first word used in turn in its definition.

In trying to avoid such a logical circle, lexicographers make the tacit assumption that certain words are more generally known than others and hence that these latter should be used in defining the former, and not the former in defining the latter.

A somewhat different but related question is whether certain words are *necessary* to the definition of other words but not vice versa? Such words would in a certain sense be more fundamental. Consider *zenith* for example. Not only is it the sort of word people will tend to look up in the dictionary, but it would seem that one cannot define it without using certain other words to express the notion of "highest point in the sky" or "point overhead." On the other hand, it does not seem that it would ever be necessary to use a word like *zenith* in defining any other word, except perhaps in a word like *nadir* to express the opposite.

These kinds of considerations might lead to the discovery of a limited number of truly fundamental words, semantic "atoms" with which all other words could be defined. In developing the notion of Basic English, C. K. Ogden tried to do something like this.[1] Using only the 850 words of Basic English in his definitions, he compiled a dictionary of 20,000 words.

These considerations lead us into the structure of vocabulary. A new way of analyzing the structure of vocabulary has been used in recent linguistics and involves the notion of distinctive features already discussed at some length in previous chapters. This method seeks an irreducible minimum of concepts (called "features") by which we may define all the lexical items of a language. It differs from previous methods in that we do not necessarily define more complex words in terms of other words in the language. Rather, we use concepts whose expression may in fact be fairly complicated when put into ordinary language. However, these concepts are *logically* simpler even if their linguistic expression is more complex. They are to be viewed as abstract elements (features) and we may indicate this by using symbols in place of words. For example, in the English kinship terminology, the sex of the person referred to is involved in the definition of all terms except *cousin* and *sibling*. Thus sex is a recurrent feature, which enters into combinations with other elements, such as generation, in a whole series of terms. We cannot just say "male" or "female" since in many systems the sex of the speaker as well as the person referred to may enter as a feature. Hence we need the basic feature "sex of person referred to," which is logically simple even though its expression in English is complex.

Analysis of vocabulary structure in terms of such underlying features and their combinations is prominent in contemporary semantic theory. An advantage is that these features tend to recur across many languages and thus tend to form a set which is universally applicable, somewhat like the features of phonology.

However, such features will not be adequate to generate definitions of all words. One reason is that we are confined to a single rather simple logical operation, namely, the and-relation, which is called in logic "conjunction." A "father" is a relative who is in the parental generation *and* is lineal *and* refers to a male person. This model may be adequate in phonology when we may define the sound of *b* in *beat* as the conjunction of a set of features such as voicing, bilabial articulation, and stop closure. In vocabulary, however, more complex operations are often necessary. Suppose, for example, we wish to define manuscripts as "written by hand." This definition cannot be reasonably expressed as a conjunction. It is not merely that something is written, *and* that the hand is employed in producing it. There is a relation between the two involved, which we might call "instrument." The manuscript is something that is written *by* hand. In a way, the definition contains an incorporated phrase. Thus, lexical semantics cannot be entirely separated from the other main branch of semantics, the problems of higher-level phrase, clause, and sentence interpretation.

Sentence interpretation semantics involves many issues. One of these has to do with the relation between syntax or grammar and semantics. It seems reasonable that the units in a sentence that are in some sense meaningful and therefore significant from the semantic point of view must also be distinguished as such in grammatical analysis. Hence many developments in syntactic analysis will affect semantic theory.

The rise of transformational grammatical theory was closely connected with semantic concerns. The view of sentences as consisting of sequences of classes of elements seemed as inadequate from the semantic as well as syntactic point of view. The crucial point was indeed a kind of ambiguity that might be called "grammatical ambiguity." Two sentences analyzable as sequences of members of the same classes and divisible at corresponding points may not represent the same basic grammatical relations necessary for understanding the sentences.

Commonly cited examples are "John is easy to please" and "John is eager to please." They are identical except for *easy* and *eager*, both of which are adjectives. Moreover, the words can be grouped in the same way when breaking down the sentence. But this does not allow us to show that in the first sentence John is semantically the object of *please*, while in the second John is the subject of *please*. In transformational theory these two sentences are derived from different "deep structures." These deep structures incorporate the grammatical relations needed for the correct interpretation of the meaning. Thus, "John is easy to please" is derived from a set of underlying, or deep-structure, sentences, in one of which John is the object ("Someone pleases John") while the other has a deep-structure sentence in which John is the subject ("John pleases someone").

In addition, increasing attention is being paid to discourse. It has been a kind of working assumption in linguistics that the sentence is the highest-level of word groupings relevant to grammatical analysis. Discourse then would be a sequence of one or more sentences each of which could autonomously be analyzed syntactically and interpreted semantically. This is a useful and even indispensable fiction because we must start with manageable units. However, there are obviously linguistically relevant relations between sentences. For example, the reference of a pronoun can sometimes only be established by going back to the previous sentence.

Also, we cannot fully describe the meaning of a sentence without reference to general presuppositions involving the interaction of speaker and hearer. Thus, in a crowded classroom, if I ask, "Will someone open a window?" which appears to be a question by formal grammatical analysis, there is a presupposition that the windows are closed. Also in this example, what is a formal question is actually a request or even a command. Many issues of this sort are now under investigation and are the subject of lively controversy in semantic theory.

Chapter 6

LINGUISTIC CHANGE

Suppose an average speaker of contemporary American English were asked to identify the language and, if possible, to translate the following sentence, written here in phonetic transcription: [ɪč nɛ ɛom wíərðɛ θæt ɪč beːo θiːn súnʊ némnɛd.][1]

If he heard someone pronounce it, he would conclude that it was some unidentifiable foreign language which he could not understand. In written form, with more time available and word divisions, he might do somewhat better.

Actually this sentence dates from about A.D. 900 and is taken from the story of the prodigal son in the Gospel according to St. Luke as translated into Old English. A reasonably colloquial idiomatic translation would be: "I don't deserve to be called your son." A more literal translation might be: "I am not worthy that I be called thy son."

From this example we can see that English has changed greatly in the course of a thousand years without, however, destroying all connection with its past. The difference is actually greater than we might think. Even words that seem to be direct ancestors of modern English forms are often not. For example, [wíərðɛ] is not the direct source of the modern *worthy*, but rather of *worth*. Forms like *worth*, which still survive in sentences like "It is worth a lot of money," were once used much more freely, so that one could produce sen-

[1] The phonetic symbols which appear here for the first time are: [ɪ] (*i* in *it*); [ɛ] (*e* in *end*); [ʊ] (*u* in *pull*). The colon indicates a long vowel. For pronunciation guide, see Appendix A.

tences whose modern equivalent would be "I am not worth to be called your son," where *worth* is used in the same way as the archaic *loth* in "I am loth to do it." In other instances, the words appear to be the same but they were embedded in a different type of grammatical system. Thus [súnʊ] 'son' had inflected forms for four cases, as we find in contemporary German, and [súnʊ] is here the nominative singular.

Though the changes in English have been extensive and involve every aspect of language—the sounds, the grammatical structure, and the meaning—they have been so gradual that if, at any particular time, people were asked about the changes in their own lifetime they would probably claim that they were minimal or even nonexistent.

The English example above could be paralleled in any language for which we have written records over an extended period. Linguistic change is a universal process. All languages are undergoing changes at all periods of their history. For this reason, the treatment of the major aspects of language in the previous three chapters was in one important respect an abstraction, a fiction based on the assumption that we could study the structure of a language as though it were a completely fixed entity rather than one which was in the process of change even while we were studying it.

Studies carried out on this assumption of fixity in the language being studied are called "synchronic linguistics," whereas the study of process of change itself belongs to "diachronic" linguistics (see Chapter 1). This division between synchronic and diachronic approaches is not, of course, confined to language. Human social systems other than linguistics, as well as physical and biological systems, can also be studied from these two different points of view.

Even though synchronic studies rest on the fiction that change is not occurring, such abstraction seems to be a necessary assumption in order to begin our study. We need a fixed and stable object for our investigation.

Let us call this fixed abstraction a "state." For example, English as spoken about A.D. 1600 is a "language state." Such states are the subject matter for ordinary descriptive grammars. When we study the history of a particular language for which documents exist, we compare successive states and make statements about the changes that have occurred. Thus, though change itself is gradual, we study it as though it consisted of instantaneous jumps from one state to the next, much like moves in a chess game. The problem is simply an example of one of the famous paradoxes of the ancient philosopher Zeno who asked how an arrow could move since at every moment it was in a different place.

Still, synchronic states exhibit evidence of the fact that what we are studying is not really stable but is in a state of flux. One of the properties of a synchronic state is variability, which is always present and derives from the simultaneous existence of older inherited forms alongside of innovations that have not yet replaced them. Changes are either incremental, decremental, or replacive. An example of incremental change is a new vocabulary item used to designate some physical invention, new social motivation, or new item of knowledge. Thus before the invention of television, a word to designate it together with certain additional terms connected with it—e.g., "teleprompter"—did not exist in the English language. Again, a form of joint ownership of a place of residence known as a "condominium" is a socioeconomic institution of recent date. An example of new knowledge is that of the New World; before the discovery of the New World, "America" and a host of other geographical terms did not exist in European languages. Such changes may be called "incremental" because they *add* new terms to the language rather than *replace* old ones.

Because of the cumulative nature of technology, we are more likely to be aware of this aspect of language than of its opposite, decremental change, or of loss without replacement. For example, English once possessed a rich vocabulary relating to such pursuits as falconry, archery, and seamanship vis-à-vis sailing ships. These have largely disappeared from general use, and what is left today is known only to very few people.

The third type of change, replacement, is by far the most common and exists in all aspects of language. For example, a rather restricted group of English nouns, to judge from dictionaries and more "conservative" speech, replace an -*f* in the singular with -*v* in the plural of nouns such as *loaf/loaves*, *calf/calves*. There is clearly a tendency in contemporary English to extend this pattern. Thus recently in a student term paper, I encountered the *rooves* as the plural of *roof* in place of standard English *roofs*. This new form is a replacement, i.e., *rooves* is used in place of an already existing form *roofs* and has the same function, i.e., to provide a plural for the singular form *roof*.

None of these three types of change occur suddenly. The incremental forms, until they have spread to the point at which they are known to virtually all the speakers of the language, will be used by some and not by others; the speech of the two groups will therefore differ in that respect. The same holds for decremental forms until they have completely disappeared.

In regard to replacives, the old and new forms will exist side by side in the speech community as a whole. Some will still use the older form while others will have adopted the innovation. There will even be variability within the speech of a single individual, who may use both forms, perhaps with disproportional frequencies or in different social situations.

Because of this variability, which is simply an aspect of ongoing change, there are difficulties in attempting to describe any single language synchronically. Uniform language is in fact a kind of fiction, however indispensable in practice. We can use it because there is still a vast body of vocabulary items and grammatical forms which are, at the moment of description, stable and common to all speakers. If this were not so, the language could not function as an instrument of communication.

Several simplifying assumptions have been made in the foregoing description of how historical change proceeds within a community of people who speak the same language. It was assumed that when one form replaces another, the ultimate triumph of the innovating form is assured. However, two other results are possible. One is that the new form may only last awhile and then disappear. This is often true of slang which rapidly passes in and out of the language. The other is that the two competing forms may develop somewhat different functions and thus both may survive alongside of each other indefinitely. For a vocabulary item, it may be a difference in meaning that develops. For example, words such as *street, avenue,* and *way* were once synonymous but have developed specialized meanings in relation to their size and importance. Again, a replacing form may establish itself alongside of the older form with particular stylistic connotations, e.g., as more or less colloquial. So various synonyms for *man*—e.g., *guy* and *fellow*—survive but with different nuances in degree of formality or informality. *Guy* also illustrates differentiation from a meaning originally synonymous with *man,* namely, its growing use in the plural to include both sexes. This is generally in the second person plural. The second person singular and plural (*you*) is anomalous in the pronoun system of English, compared to almost all other languages, in that it does not distinguish number.

Ideas about the spread of new and disappearance of older speech forms were also oversimplified in the earlier discussion where it was assumed that an incremental or a replacive form would eventually spread to all the speakers of the language and that a decremental form would disappear in the same manner.

However, suppose that one of these changes does not spread to the entire population speaking the language, even after a long period. That this might happen for vocabulary innovations relating to the specialized terminology of a particular occupational group—e.g., carpenters or lawyers—is not difficult to see. Insofar as a society has certain barriers, new forms arising within a particular group may repeatedly tend to remain confined to that group, and forms from outside the group will tend not to be adopted by it. The consequence is the formation of "dialects," definite coherent varieties with a whole series of distinct idiosyncratic features characteristic of subgroups within the total population which speaks the language.

The term "dialect" is used in linguistics somewhat differently than it is in general speech, in which "dialect" designates a spoken variety as against a standardized written form of the general language. In the linguistic use of this term, every language is a group of dialects. Indeed, a language is the totality of dialects which are mutually intelligible.

In the history of the human race, by far the most important barrier to communication which has given rise to distinct dialects is geographical. Hence we talk of geographical or regional dialects.

There is a point at which distinct dialects become so different from each other that their speakers can no longer understand each other. Once such a point is reached we can talk of distinct languages, but they, of course, still show numerous similarities which result from their origin as dialectical varieties of the same language. We say that they are "related languages." For example, English, German, Dutch, and the Scandinavian languages were once dialects of a single language. About A.D. 500 they were probably still mutually intelligible.

The significance of this phenomenon of divergence for historical and comparative linguistics is one to which we will return later. Let us now turn back to the example at the beginning of the chapter, which is repeated here for convenience.

[ɪč nɛ ɛom wíǝrðɛ θæt ɪč be:o θi:n súnʊ némnɛd.]

Let us consider the first word [ɪč] which meant *I* and was pronounced approximately like the Modern English word *itch*. In a somewhat complicated sense, the Modern English *I* [aj] is the descendant of this form. But to understand what happened in between requires reference to local dialect variation as well as to certain social and demographic factors and more purely linguistic considerations.

Old English had well-marked regional dialects. The document from which the above sentence was taken was written in the dialect which formed the basis of the literary language and is hence the form of Old English found in most of the surviving documents of this period. This was the West Saxon dialect. In this dialect an earlier *k* sound had become *ch* [č] after front vowels like [ɪ] (as in *hit*). However, the dialects farther north, Mercian (Midlands) and Northumbrian, did not participate in this change. Hence in these dialects one said [ɪk], just as one does, for example, in Modern Dutch and the Low German dialects of northern Germany now.

For several centuries the northern and southern dialects went their separate ways. The south said [ɪč], while the north said [ɪk]. But in the north during this period a further change occurred. The *k* was dropped before a following word beginning with a consonant but retained before a vowel. These were thus two variant forms, much like the two forms of the Modern English indefinite article, which has *a* before consonants and *an* before vowels. Thus, one said in the north [i:brɪ́ŋgɛ] 'I bring', with a long vowel somewhat like the modern vowel in the word *see*, but [ɪké:tɛ] 'I eat'.

After 1400 the form [i:] began to replace [ɪk] before vowels so that, again in the north, one began to say [i:ete] 'I eat'. This process is called analogy. Speakers began to use [i:] before a vowel on the analogy of its use before a consonant.

To understand the subsequent changes, certain historical events need to be considered. The Old English literary language was based on West Saxon. With the Norman Conquest in 1066, French became the predominant literary language. During the Middle English period (1150–1450) English gradually re-emerged as a literary language but under strong French influence, particularly in vocabulary. The dialects of Middle English could still be divided roughly into southern and northern, though the boundaries between them and the further subdivisions of the two main areas were by that time somewhat different. Unlike the Old English period there was no single literary standard in the Middle English period. By the fifteenth century, however, the London dialect began to dominate and ultimately became the basis for the standard English.

The speech of London itself was southern but on the border of the northern dialect. About this time, in the fifteenth century, northern migrants came to London in large numbers and began to affect its speech. One of the results was the replacement of southern [ɪč] by northern [i:]. The old southern form may still be found, however, in local rural dialects of southern England.

This northern form [i:] is the direct ancestor of standard Modern English *I*, pronounced [aj]. However, its pronunciation has changed from that of the vowel in Modern English *see* to that of Modern English *sigh*. The change from [i:] to [aj] (symbolized [i: >aj]) in this word was not an isolated one. It was but one of numerous instances of what is called a "regular sound shift," or, sometimes, "sound law." Almost every word that had the [i:] sound changed it to [aj] over an extended period beginning in the fifteenth century. Thus Middle English [rīdan] became modern *ride*, [bītan] became *bite*, etc. A further example of this change is shown by our sentence: the form [θi:n] became Modern (now archaic) English *thine*. The spelling of these words has not changed. In Middle and Old English the letter *i* was used to symbolize the phonetic value [i:] as in Modern English *see*, because this was the value of *i* in Latin at the time the Latin alphabet was adopted and this is still its phonetic value in French and Italian, among other languages.

In fact, this change [i: >aj] was but part of an even larger set of changes known as the "great vowel shift," by which a large part of the Middle English system was transformed basically into Modern English. These then are the basic facts about the complicated process by which Old English form [ič] gave rise to modern [aj], 'I'.

Any explanation of linguistic change must take note of two very different kinds of factors. One might be termed "external," or "sociolinguistic," that is, the existence of certain dialects in Old English with certain boundaries conformed to certain social facts since each of the dialect areas was a distinct political and cultural entity whose boundaries were an inhibiting factor in the spread of linguistic forms. Again, the importance of the speech of London to the development of the modern standard form of English and of the migrations in the late Middle Ages of northern speakers into London are nonlinguistic, i.e., social, economic, and political, facts without which the whole development cannot be understood.

Yet if we ask why in southern English the *k* sound became the *ch* sound as in *church* after a front vowel, we cannot even begin to understand this without a consideration of the physiological aspect of the articulations involved. There are four changes undergone by *I* mentioned above, which can be classified as internal or linguistic rather than external or socio-linguistic. These four changes are: (1) the change from [k] to [č] after the front vowel [ɪ] in the southern dialect of Old English; (2) the loss of *k* before consonants that produced the variants [i:] and [ɪk] in the northern dialect; (3) the replacement of [ɪk] by [i:] in the northern dialect; and (4) the change in the pronunciation from [i:] to [aj] in the transitional period.

The first of these, namely the change from [k] to [č] after front vowels, is an example of what is called a "regular conditioned" sound change—"regular" because it affected all instances of *k* after a front vowel in whatever words it was found and "conditioned" because it only occurred when front vowels (i.e., vowels produced by raising the front of the tongue) were involved. In this respect it contrasts with the fourth change, namely, [i: >aj], which affected *all* instances of the vowel [i:] and is hence called an "unconditioned" sound change.

The fact that the earlier change *was* conditioned suggests that the condition under which it occurred is an important factor. This condition was the occurrence of a front vowel before the *k* while *k* remained if it was preceded by a back vowel. A *k* sound is produced as we have seen by making a closure of the vocal passage with the back of the tongue against the velum, or soft palate. An adjacent back vowel such as *o* or *u* is also produced by raising this same part of the tongue toward the soft palate. There is thus a harmony of position and the same part of the tongue is involved. But if the vowel is a front one, it is the front part of the tongue which is involved and so there is a disharmony. One common result is that the articulation of the *k* is moved forward in varying degrees. In this case it ultimately produced a *ch* sound which involves a part of the tongue that is further forward than that employed in articulating *k*.

Such a change is called "palatalization" and it has occurred frequently in many different languages in different periods,

For example, in modern Italian the former k sound of Latin has changed to *ch* (spelled *c*, before front vowels).

Such a conditional change belongs to the very large class of assimilative sound changes, so-called because a sound, after the change, is more like the sound which conditioned it than before. The k acquired a front articulation which is more like the following front vowel. Such changes obviously involve an elimination of certain articulatory movements. After the change takes place, it is no longer necessary to change the tongue from a position in which the back is raised to one in which the front is raised. Such assimilatory phonetic changes are much more frequent than the opposite, dissimilatory kind, in which they become more unlike.

The second change was where in the dialects which retained k, this k was dropped before a following consonant but not before a vowel. Unlike the previous change it was sporadic, not regular, because it did not occur in general in words that end in k but only in the word [ɪk]. Though most changes are regular in the sense that they occur in all words which satisfy specified phonetic conditions, words such as pronouns may undergo irregular changes. Even here there is a general principle at work. The k in this case was lost before another consonant but not before a vowel. It is generally found in languages that consonant sequences, or clusters, particularly of certain types, are unstable. Yet a single consonant followed by a vowel, as in [ɪk e:tɛ] 'I eat', is a very "natural" sequence in that syllables consisting of a single consonant followed by a single vowel are found in all languages and such syllables are the first type to occur in children's speech, e.g., *mama* and *papa*.

The third change, that by which the [i:] form replaced the [ɪk] form even before vowels, is of a different type from the ones we have considered up to now. It is an example of a widespread group of changes called "analogical" changes. When the same word or morpheme has more than one phonetic form, speakers tend to use one form at the expense of the others, which ultimately results in less irregularity in the grammatical structure of the language. In this instance the variation between [i:] and [ɪk] originally resulted from a simplification of articulation, in that *k* was dropped before a consonant. This grammatical complication was destroyed by analogical change. When children make up a plural *tooths*, they are similarly carrying out analogical change. If *tooths* and other plurals in English all came to end in -*s*, then the variation in the plural morpheme would be destroyed and the plurals would all be regular. In fact, the -*s* plural has spread throughout the history of English. In Old English there were many different ways of forming the plural. For example, one common variant involved the addition of -*n* which has only survived in *oxen* and *children*. In this last word *n* was added to an old plural in -*r*.

The fourth change, [i:>aj], was a regular conditioned change. It occurred in a very large number of words regardless of the meaning and grammatical forms involved, as do most regular sound changes. This relative independence and autonomy of change in phonetics is just one more indication of how fundamental the division is between phonology and grammar.

The change [i:>aj] is but one of a number of changes of vowels that make up the great vowel shift. Such changes involve the notion of structure in their explanation. The vowel system of any language has a systematic over-all structure in terms of recurrent features, as we discussed in Chapter 2. After a set of changes, the new system must also be structurally coherent if it is to conform to the general principle that phonological systems are organized structures. This implies that the changes must themselves to some extent be systematic, to form a coherent system. A discussion of just a part of this systematic change, as shown in Figure 8, will give an indication of what such changes are like.

	Front	Back
High	[i:] > [aj]	[u:] > [aw]
Mid	[e:] > [i:]	[o:] > [u:]

Figure 8.

What does the change from [i:] to [aj] mean in articulatory terms? The [i:] (pronounced like the *ee* in *beet*) as a long vowel in the highest front position involves a rapid rise of the front part of the tongue and then the holding of it in that position for an extended period. The tendency set in to make this rise gradually from the lowest position, that of *a*. The result was a rising motion of the tongue (a so-called rising diphthong) from the *a* to the *i* position (like the sound of the diphthong [aj] as the *i* in *bite*). A parallel tendency occurred at the same time with regard to the [u] (like the *oo* in *boot*), the highest back vowel. The result was correspondingly a diphthong moving from *a* to *u* (like the vowel sound in house). The second parts of [aj] and [aw] are simply the nonsyllabic resultants of the [i] and [u] vowel preceded by the more open and sonorant *a* which becomes the center of the syllable. Once these two changes occurred there was a gap in the systems. Since [i:] and [u:] no longer existed, speakers were free to raise the next lower vowels [e:] (pronounced like *ay* in *day*) and [o:] (pronounced like *oa* in *boat*) to produce a fuller use of the low–high dimension of vowels. Thus [e:] became [i:] and [o:] became [u:]. This is still reflected in English spelling, e.g., *meet* and *boat*. These were but the initial changes in a whole series of chain reactions that went on for several centuries and resulted in a new, systematic but different, structure from that of earlier English.

We have gone into some detail in regard to phonetic changes. A comparison of our sentence in Old English with that of Modern English, shows, however, other changes which have no reference to phonetics at all.

Several of these may be briefly mentioned in order to give some notion of other types of changes. The word [θi:n] 'thine' has been replaced by "your" in Modern English. This has nothing to do with sound changes but much to do with the change of social structure. In Old English [θi:n] and related forms like [θu:] 'thou' (modern *thou*) were used in the singular, while [e:ow] 'you' and related forms were used in the plural. During the feudal period, paralleling similar changes on the Continent, the plural began to be used by the lower classes in speaking to the upper classes as a sign of respect. Among the upper classes, to begin with, the plural was used by people who did not know each other well, while the singular was used within the family and with close friends.

Later, with democratization *you* became in general the sign of social unfamiliarity regardless of class and *thou* of intimacy. By 1700 the original plural was used everywhere except in religious language in relation to the Deity. Even this has now changed and recent Bible translations use *you*.

Finally, as an example of still another process, the word form [némnɛd] 'named' has been replaced in Modern English in this particular usage by *called*. The verb *call* was borrowed from the Northmen who invaded England from Scandinavia in the early Middle Ages. In Swedish *call* is still *kalla*.

From the foregoing discussion we see that the process of linguistic change in English is very complex, that it affects all aspects of language, and that it involves physiological factors as in phonetic change, psychological factors as in analogical change, and social factors as in the replacement of *thou* by *you*. Finally, although it involves much that might seem capricious and unpredictable, it does exhibit certain general principles of linguistic change which exist at all times and in all places.

Chapter 7

LANGUAGE AND CULTURE

Language is only one aspect of culture. Like culture it can be understood by looking either at human differences or at human similarities. These different perspectives can be expressed in English by our use of count nouns or mass nouns. As a count noun, *language* or *culture* may take a definite article. We talk of *the cultures* of particular peoples or of *the languages* they speak. These nouns in these contexts can be counted, i.e., we can ask how many cultures and languages are found in the world. In another use, as a mass noun, we talk of *culture* or *language* in general and we concentrate on basic and universal principles that transcend specific differences. However different individual cultures are from each other, humans alone organize into groups which *have* cultures. Therefore, humans must have the biological capacity for "culture" in the mass sense. This means that all human beings are capable of acquiring the particular version of human cultures that are characteristic of the groups into which they are born. This is also true of language. All humans have the general ability to acquire "language," but the specific languages they learn will be those of the group in which they are brought up.

All cultures, in spite of their great differences from each other in particular features, show a general resemblance in what might be called the "ground plan of culture." For example, all societies have rules regarding incest and some form of the family as a basic unit for socialization of the child. They all have socially organized relationships for producing and exchanging goods. They all have limitations on permitted behavior in terms of custom and law, and so on.

A further proof of general human similarity is the phenomenon known as "cultural diffusion," i.e., when specific traits of culture are taken over and assimilated by the members of one society from another. Language is one trait of culture that is subject to cultural diffusion; not only can one language borrow words from another but, within certain limits, language contact can even affect deeper structural levels of phonologic and grammatical systems. We saw an example of this with the pronoun *I* whose history was influenced by the contact among different regional groups in England.

As anthropology has progressed, anthropologists have become increasingly aware of these common features and have sought to discover their specific nature and what they can tell us about that vague but important concept "human nature."

Language is one of these basic human cultural universals. All known human groups have complex languages which exhibit essential similarities in their over-all structure. It was once thought that peoples with extremely simple technologies, so-called primitives, must have languages of a more rudimentary type than those of the more technologically advanced peoples. This turns out not to hold at all for grammar. It is true, of course, that with scientific and technical advance comes a flood of technical terminology, but languages of pre-industrial and even preagricultural peoples have a rich vocabulary in matters having to do with their external environment (e.g., plant and animal species) and nuances of emotion and interpersonal relationships.

The most important proof of human cultural similarity is that languages all exhibit certain basic structural traits, so that the techniques of scientific linguistics are applicable to all languages.

Our capacity for culture must have evolved over the vast period of five million years, during which man's development diverged from that of our relatives, the anthropoid apes. When we speak of man in this connection we are not talking exclusively about our own species, *Homo sapiens,* which took its present form perhaps 100,000 years ago, but rather of the whole group of prehistoric hominids whose physical and cultural remains provide the evidence for the complex developments which led to modern man.

Just when along this line of evolution a particular organism had the capacity for speech, we don't really know.

Moreover, how can we ask how old language is or whether it has developed from any concrete nonlinguistic antecedents until we have settled in our mind what the defining characteristics of language itself are?

While there is no single answer everyone would agree on, the very lack of agreement stems from an encouraging fact. Human language is so rich and complex that we can identify a number of characteristics, any one of which could be taken to be definitional. One of them, for example, is duality, i.e., the existence in language of two levels, a phonological and a grammatical. This characteristic of articulate speech allows us to devise thousands of meaningful units from a very limited number of phonological units, providing the basis for the enormous vocabularies of human languages. Another is the existence of a theoretical infinity of grammatical sentences. These and other definitional features of language are important to the questions we have about the origin of language.

Human language is so much more complex than the communication systems of other species, even the signals used by our closest biological relatives, the anthropoid apes in their natural state, that we must wonder whether language evolved by a series of steps from some other nonlinguistic system in a sound medium or whether it evolved from a completely fresh beginning. The first of these views may be labeled the "continuity" and the second the "discontinuity" view.

The recent and highly publicized experiments in teaching "languages" to chimpanzees and other higher primates has tipped the balance toward a continuity theory. While the performances of these animals lack some of the basic characteristics of human language (such as the use of the sound medium, duality of structure, and infinity of expression) and while they did not develop spontaneously but were taught by experimenters, they indicate the presence of a general symbolic capacity which may not be very different from that of the earliest hominids. It also shows that the purely physical development of the human speech apparatus is very important. Real success with chimpanzees only appeared when communication was transposed from a sound to a visual medium—deaf and dumb signs or counters on a board. But visual systems have built in functional limitations. They can't be used at night or at a distance, and they require the use of the hands which during verbal communication are free to do other things. The anthropologist Jane Hill cogently observes that "the cognitive capacities of chimpanzees have been elicited by teaching them communication systems involving the use of hands, and it is clear that any wild chimpanzee who spent a lot of time doing deaf signs or moving blocks on a board would soon be a very dead chimpanzee."[2]

When and in what species do we find the first system that exhibits the properties of language? Well, language is at least as old as our own species which is only about 100,000 years old. But the idea that language is a "recent" acquisition has only become popular in the last several years. An older view, recently revived, dates language from millions of years ago, to fossil forms more primitive than *Homo sapiens*, such as *Homo erectus*. This view makes language coincident with the very earliest of tool-making traditions.

Two human capacities have always been called basic to human cultural evolution: language and tool making. The British naturalist Jane Goodall's observations of primates in Africa show that elementary tools are made spontaneously by nonhuman primates. But no true human linguistic communication has been found. The reader may well ask why we think of language as the *sine qua non* of culture. Well, for one reason, language gives us the means to classify our natural and social environment. For example, incest rules require language. For example, for many peoples, marriage between parallel cousins, i.e., children of two full sisters or two full brothers is forbidden, while marriage between cross-cousins, i.e., between the child of a brother and the child of a sister, is favored. Such

[2] Jane Hill, "On the Evolutionary Foundation of Language," *American Anthropologist* 74:3 (June 1972), 308–17.

a rule is obviously impossible for dogs or even chimpanzees, who lack the linguistic means by which such classification might be developed.

Another basic function of language is the transmission of nonlinguistic culture. The continuity and elaboration through time of separate human traditions would seem to depend on language as the essential means for instruction in and the transmission of accumulated knowledge.

Finally, much of human culture is itself linguistic, taking fixed verbal forms, both spoken and written. This includes literature, religious, and legal systems, expressions of cultural values as found in proverbs, etc. Coherent ideologies without language are impossible. Shared values that can be stated are necessary to all societies.

The "origin of language" has also been understood in terms of the nature of the "original" language of mankind. Scholars have wondered whether there was a single original language, and, if it existed, what it was like compared to existing languages today.

Sadly enough, our knowledge of even the most extensive and remote historical relationships does not permit us to link all the major linguistic stocks of the world in such a way as to give a complete genealogy of languages going back to the protohuman (meaning proto-*Homo sapiens*), since the language of any of the *Homo erectus* or other fossil human forms is not recoverable.

We also have no way of knowing what the earlier, if not earliest, languages were like. However, the kind of protolanguage of large stocks like Indo-European, which we can reconstruct by the methods of historical linguistics, and the earliest written languages like those of ancient Egypt reveal linguistic structures which are not basically different from those of contemporary languages. This same structural similarity holds for languages of contemporary preliterates.

These facts upset widely held notions concerning the evolution of language from simpler to more complex structures which were held by many nineteenth-century linguists and linger on today in other fields. As far back as we can go, language has been language as we know it now, with all the basic properties of existing languages.

Having made the distinction between "language" and "languages" and, correspondingly, on "culture" and "cultures" in most of this chapter, we have been concerned only with the former of these pairs, that is, the relationship of language in general to culture in general. The relationship of the second member of each pair is also an important matter and raises the following questions. To what extent do linguistic differences and cultural differences correlate? For example, given certain facts about a specific language, could we predict certain other facts about the nonlinguistic aspects of a specific culture? If such correlations exist, what are they like and how extensive are they? Further, which is the causal factor? Do the differences in languages cause the differences in cultures or is it the other way around? Or is the relation perhaps more complicated, involving a sort of give-and-take between the two sets of factors?

In vocabulary there are real and obvious correlations of this sort. For example, the dictionary of a language reflects quite strongly a people's knowledge of its natural environment and social institutions and its judgment of the relative importance of different aspects of them. The numerous Eskimo words for different kinds of snow and ice and the vast Arabic terminology relating to camels are celebrated examples. Again, there is generally some correlation between kinship terminology and family and clan institutions. For example, there are certain clans in which membership is patrilineally determined, i.e., the child always belongs to the father's group (as in the inheritance of family names) and other ethnic groups in which there is a matrilineal rule by which children always belong to the mother's group. In some instances the kinship terminology even overrides generational lines and is largely based on such matrilineal or patrilineal groupings. For example, in a terminology called by anthropologists the "Crow" type, because it is used by the Crow Indians, among others, various male members of a person's matrilineal group have the same kin term applied to them regardless of generation. Socially, the Crow have matrilineal groups.

Whereas this kind of correlation between kinship terminology and certain aspects of social life often exists, there are also many instances in which there is no such relationship. The features of terminology in these cases appear to be no more than arbitrary choices, historically conditioned, among the logically possible systems of classification.

However, the existence of many undoubted correspondences between vocabulary and other cultural features has led some thinkers to postulate a far more thoroughgoing relationship extending beyond vocabulary to other aspects of language, e.g., grammatical categories. In its extreme form, this view has been called either "linguistic relativity," "linguistic world view," or "linguistic determinism." It has been most persuasively advanced by an American linguist, Benjamin Whorf, and for this reason this doctrine has sometimes been called "Whorfianism." In a paper entitled "The Relation of Habitual Thought and Behavior to Language," he states as his main aim the investigation of the following question: "Are our own concepts of 'time,' 'space,' and 'matter' given by experience to all men, or are they in part determined by the structure of the particular language?"[3] The conclusion to which he comes in this paper is the following: "Concepts of 'time' and 'matter' are not given in substantially the same form by experience to all men but depend on the nature of the language or languages through the use of which they have developed" —hence the term "linguistic relativity," used by Whorf during a period when Einstein's theory of relativity had a considerable influence on general patterns of thought. Our concepts are asserted to be "relative" to the particular language which we speak. The term "linguistic world view" ("linguistic Weltanschauung") suggests another aspect of this theory. It is not only particular concepts that are derived from our language

[3] Benjamin Lee Whorf, "The Relation of Habitual Thought and Behavior to Language," in *Language, Thought and Reality: Selected Writings*, ed. by John B. Carroll (Cambridge, Mass.: Technology Press Book, Massachusetts Institute of Technology Press, 1958), pp. 134–59.

but also a coherent way of looking at the world, a philosophy, as it were, which will differ from language to language. The third term for this approach, "linguistic determinism," indicates the fact that although Whorf at times seems to qualify his statements, he does assign to language the dominant causal role in producing a particular world view.

Whorf's own more specific theories derive largely from contrast between the Hopi Indian language and English and other languages of Western Europe, which he believes to be essentially similar and which he therefore calls "SAE" (standard average European).

Whorfian theories have understandably fascinated many professional scientists, particularly psychologists and cultural anthropologists, and many nonprofessionals as well. However, those investigating their validity have encountered great difficulty in stating these theories in a precise form and subjecting them to scientific testing.

One difficulty with Whorfianism has been raised, particularly by philosophers, on the following question: If in fact our language does determine our mode of thought, how can Whorf, whose language is English and whose thinking is therefore by his own admission determined by English, transcend this limitation, discover the different Hopi categories, and then state his results in English so they can be understood by others presumably subject to the same limitations?

Another basic problem has been that in large part Whorf's reasoning has been circular. World view has been derived from linguistic categories which are then said to prove the existence of this same world view which has derived from the linguistic categories in the first place. This can be illustrated from the following example, imaginary in that nobody has used it, but based on real linguistic facts and paralleling in form a type of reasoning very common in these cases:

All languages with a system of cardinal numerals that go beyond the first few make use of a recurrent mathematical base. This is most commonly, as in our own system, 10. Thus for us, "326" is expressed in words as "three hundred twenty-six" and thus is equivalent to $3 \times 10^2 + 2 \times 10 + 6$. Such a system is called a "decimal" system since it is based on multiples of ten (Latin, *decimus,* tenth) and powers of ten. Other cultures use a different numerical base, for example, 20; a base 20 system is called "vigesimal" (Latin, *vigesimus,* twentieth). Suppose now we say that peoples with the former type system have a "decimal" world view while the latter have a "vigesimal" world view. What is the evidence for this? The answer is the numerical systems themselves.

In order to avoid this sort of circularity, we must relate the linguistic categories to evidence that is independent of language. This is obviously very difficult. If we resort, for instance, to psychological experiments, in most experimental situations language will intervene in the subject's responses.

In recent years attempts to test and give empirical content to Whorfian ideas have concentrated on experiments with color terminology. Here the results have tended to be negative. A recent book on color terminologies which has attracted wide attention is that of Berlin and Kay.[4] What they have discovered and what has apparently survived the numerous detailed critiques of their work is the following: Across languages, the division of the color spectrum in terms of the three standard variables—hue, brightness, and saturation—is far from arbitrary. A few recurrent boundaries define the color terms of all languages. Some languages recognize more of these boundaries than others, i.e., have more color terms, but the boundaries themselves are very similar across languages.

They also discovered that there is a further and remarkable constraint on the possible number of color terminologies. For example, even languages with the simplest color systems of all, i.e., those with two basic color words, always have the same essential division—that between "black," embracing all the darker colors, and "white," embracing all the light ones—and with close to identical boundaries in all cases. In less simple color systems, if a third color is added, it is always red; a fourth color is always yellow or green; and if there are five colors, they are always black, white, red, yellow, and green, and so on. The number of color systems is therefore remark-

[4] Brent Berlin and P. Kay, *Basic Color Terms, Their Universality and Evolution* (Berkeley: University of California Press), 1969.

ably small in relation to the infinite possibilities afforded by purely arbitrary division, and the same type of system recurs again and again in different parts of the world.

In general, recent work on universal aspects of language have tended to reveal similar limitations whether we are looking at vocabulary, grammatical categories, or sound systems. Our common human nature and the relatively uniform conditions required for human communication everywhere reduce the number of possible systems to a relatively restricted and constantly recurring set.

Chapter 8

LANGUAGE AND SOCIETY

Culture and society are correlative concepts. The population units with which social science deals at various levels, such as tribes, local communities, nations, etc., can be considered from two points of view. The first is predicated on the fact that all members of a particular unit share certain distinctive patterns of behavior, beliefs, and values which constitute their culture. However, each unit can also be viewed as comprising individuals with recurrent ways of interacting with other individuals, appropriate to their roles within organized social groupings such as families, labor unions, or political parties.

Language is as fundamental to the organization of a society or a group as it is to the expression of its culture, for language is primarily social. A language confined to one person is either an instance of the survival of the last living speaker of a previous community or a pathological case. A language is a code common to many people by which they interact. In fact, the very possession of a common code is an important basis for solidarity among members of a group. "He speaks my language" implies more than just the capacity for exchanging information.

Recently, in recognition of the practical and scientific importance of this field, sociolinguistics has become an autonomous study. Because this is a new and rapidly expanding interdisciplinary field, there are considerable differences of opinion about its precise definition and scope. Therefore, instead of giving a formal definition of it, it may be more useful if I distinguish the following main areas of concern, which suggest the range of questions that concern sociolinguists: (1) linguistic variability within speech communities in terms of social class, ethnicity, occupation, sex, etc.; (2) variability within the individual speaker in the course of his social interaction, which we might call his "repertoire"; (3) the relation of speech variants to group identity; and (4) matters of policy and planning in the area of language.

A concept basic to sociolinguistics is the "speech community," which is a group of people who habitually interact with each other linguistically. In every speech community there are a number of speech variants. These may be very similar linguistically and thus merely varieties of the same language. But often they involve completely different or even historically unrelated varieties. Every individual commands one or more of these variants. Particularly striking examples exist in India where various occupational castes within a single community may speak very different languages from each other and where such multilingualism may last over centuries.

The speech community must be carefully distinguished from the language community. An example of a language community is the set of all speakers of English. They may be said to belong to the same language community insofar as there is potential mutual intelligibility through the use of some form of English. We say "potential" because by this conception, the English language community includes, for example, speakers of English in Australia and the United States who are unlikely to interact linguistically very often. For this reason, within sociolinguistics it is the speech community rather than the language community that is the basic unit of study.

Every speech community is an organized system in that it possesses a certain set of speech variants that are coherently distributed within the population and are used in relatively fixed patterns. We can investigate language along several dimensions. First is the linguistic range. To what extent are the variants of a language similar forms of the same language and to what extent are they distinct languages? What are the linguistic characteristics of each of the variants? Next is the dimension of function. How do factors such as physical setting and social situation affect the choice of variants? For example, in the German-speaking areas of Switzerland there are two main linguistic variants, the local dialects of Swiss German and the standardized literary form of German (High German). The functions of these two languages are differentiated to the point where the use of one rather than the other in certain situations would be highly inappropriate and produce strong reactions. Thus, a professor always lectures in Standard German, but if he chats with a student after class it will probably be in Swiss German unless the student is a foreigner who is unfamiliar with it.

The topic of conversation also influences a person's choice among variants. Two Swiss-German professors outside of the classroom situation are likely to use Standard German if they are discussing technical subjects, but Swiss German if they are discussing personal affairs.

Where, as with Swiss and Standard German, the two types of speech are forms of the same language, the situation is known to linguists as "diglossia." Other examples are Creole French as against Standard French in Haiti, Classical Arabic as against the many vernaculars in the Arabic speaking world, and black English as against Standard English for many black speakers in the United States.

A single overarching variable is evident in all of these examples: the opposition between, or, more often, a continuum ranging from, formality to casualness. The variant used in formal situations is characteristically more prestigious. It is often a form that has a written standard, while the casual variant may rarely or never be used in writing.

Another important distinction in speech communities can be made between dialects, such as Swiss-German, and superposed variants. The former are in some sense more fundamental than the latter. Two speech varieties are different dialects if they differ in a whole series of structural characteristics embracing phonology, grammar, and vocabulary. They may indeed be quite separate and unrelated languages and are very commonly defined by locality. They are generally acquired as first languages or very early in life and are often the reference point for ethnic identity.

Superposed variants are generally acquired later and differ from the language norm only in restricted and relatively superficial ways. Examples of these are adolescent slang and the linguistic peculiarities which set apart certain occupational groups. Typically, the differences in these cases affect only certain aspects of the vocabulary.

One example of a superposed variant is lawyer's speech. It has become usual for English-speaking lawyers, in pronouncing the word *defendant*, to use an unreduced vowel in the last syllable so that it rhymes with the word *ant* rather than with the last syllable of words like *tangent, contingent*, etc. Lawyers also use *peremptory* as a noun, meaning a "peremptory challenge" to a prospective juror, i.e., one of a certain number who can be disqualified without giving a reason.

In addition to dialects and superposed variants, there is a third type of variation of a language, which linguistically is the most superficial. An example of this is the use of both the *tu* (singular) and *vous* (plural) for the second person singular pronoun in French, a difference found in many languages and including at one time English (*thou* and *you*). It is obviously part of their acquired knowledge of their own language for French speakers to use the "intimate" (*tu*) and "polite" (*vous*) forms appropriately. When a French speaker uses one or the other in a sentence, he or she is not speaking a different dialect or even a superposed variant because it is part of the knowledge of *all* French speakers beyond a very early age. However, the use of "T and V forms," as they are called, is largely regulated by the same factor—formality versus casualness—that in other societies governs the choice of dialects or standard languages.

In a classic study, Brown and Gilman have shown that there are two variables in the T and V case—power and intimacy.[1] The V form, a plural, was originally used asym-

[1] Roger W. Brown and A. Gilman, "The Pronouns of Power and Solidarity," in Thomas A. Sebeok, ed., *Style in Language* (Cambridge, Mass.: Technology Press Book, Massachusetts Institute of

metrically—i.e., members of the lower class used it in speaking to the upper class while the upper class used T form to the lower class. There is also a factor of intimacy; the upper-class members used the V form with each other when they were strangers but always used the T form with members of their own family. Gradually, with the blurring of class differences, T began to express intimacy and V formality regardless of class. Thus, in speaking French today, two acquaintances may shift from V to T as they develop a more intimate relationship.

In English, while we no longer have this distinction, since only *you* exists, the use of personal first names as against last names with titles of address (e.g., "Tom" v. "Mr. X") falls along much the same continuum and is found to be very systematic.

Beyond the basic contrast between first names and the simple titles of address, the system is complicated by the use of kinship terms and honorific titles. Thus personal names are used with friends and family members on the same or lower age or generational levels, while kinship terms for most Americans are used to address senior relatives. Ordinary titles of address (Mr., Ms., etc.) are used with casual acquaintances who are on the same level or strangers whose status is unknown, while honorific titles (Doctor, Professor, Governor) are used to indicate respect for the addressees' positions. Thus power and intimacy are combined in various ways.

But what of the dialects? On what kinds of social differentiation are they based; what factors maintain them over time? For such thoroughgoing differences as characterize dialects, powerful social isolation mechanisms must be at work. In speech communities, these mechanisms include geographical region, social class, occupation (or, as in India, castes), or religious affiliation.

In the past the geographical distinction has been by far the most potent factor in determining dialectal differences.

Technology Press, 1960), pp. 253–76. (The factor called "intimacy" here is what they call "solidarity.")

When linguists today use the term "dialect" without qualification, they too refer to a regionally defined dialect. It is not merely that geography is the most powerful factor—it is the only factor able to produce differences of such a scale that they affect all aspects of language in a region and may ultimately lead to the differentiation of separate languages from what was originally a single one. The other factors are only strong enough to maintain for varying periods of time a difference that originated from geographical separation.

For example, in some Near Eastern speech communities where dialect varieties are forms of Arabic, those spoken by various groups are different for different religious affiliations. In a classic study, Haim Blanc, doing language research in Baghdad, found three forms of Arabic exhibiting a full range of linguistic differences in phonology and grammar, spoken by Moslems, Christians, and Jews.[2] However, the evidence of history as well as that of the distribution of Arabic dialects elsewhere in the Near East, demonstrates that these dialects originated in different geographical areas and that their present juxtaposition is the result of migration to Baghdad. These differences are now maintained and strengthened by the social barriers among the three religious communities.

Similarly the caste-differentiated dialects of communities in India are based on varying regional origin followed by migration.

This difference in dialect based on geographical origin is particularly obvious when the forms of speech in the community are completely different and mutually unintelligible languages. For example, in early medieval England the upper class spoke a form of Norman French while the lower class spoke Anglo-Saxon (Old English). The mingling of the two into Middle English became the forerunner of present-day English. These two forms of language did not of course arise on the spot from an isolation mechanism involving social classes. French was brought in by the Norman nobles from

[2] Haim Blanc, *Communal Dialects in Baghdad,* Harvard Middle Eastern Monographs, No. 10 (Cambridge, Mass.: Harvard University Press, 1964).

France as a result of their conquest of England in 1066. Eventually, of course, Norman French died out but not until it had profoundly influenced Anglo-Saxon particularly in the area of vocabulary.

It is interesting to look at the mechanisms by which speech communities that are linguistically heterogeneous deal with that situation and eventually restore a degree of homogeneity. In linguistically heterogeneous speech communities, there is always widespread bilingualism or even multilingualism. The bilingualism is almost always asymmetrical, in that the speakers of one language tend to be bilingual in the other but not vice versa. There is evidently a kind of power relation between languages which is only rarely one of complete equality. Among the factors which make one language dominant are superiority in numbers, the possession of political power, and higher economic status or the fact that it has the prestige of a standard written form and the advantage of a definite governmental policy of spreading its use.

If all the speakers of a subordinate language are bilingual, that language is in danger since it can be lost in the next generation, and many languages in the course of human history have died out in this way. However, the race is not always to the swift nor the battle to the strong. Language tends to become the focus of feelings of ethnic identity, and speakers may consciously seek to preserve it. Such European minority groups as the Welsh, in Great Britain, and the Basques, particularly in Spain, put great stress on the preservation of their language, for without it they would soon lose their ethnic distinctiveness.

It is not necessary for one language to win out over the others in a speech community. Where social isolating mechanisms in the community are strong, particularly formal or informal barriers to intermarriage such as in caste-conscious India or among the religious communities in the Near East, a stable bilingualism or multilingualism may result that can last for centuries.

One common and important phenomenon regarding regional bilingualism has not yet been considered. Often a language from outside the community itself, one that is a second language for everyone who uses it, becomes the most important means by which speakers with different first-language backgrounds communicate. Such a language is called an "auxiliary language" or a "lingua franca."

Auxiliary languages, except for such artificial inventions of limited success as Esperanto, are natural languages that have often spread far beyond their original boundaries, for example, through trade. Sometimes the number of people who speak them as second languages is far greater than the number of first-language speakers. An example is Swahili, a Bantu language used in Tanzania, Kenya, and elsewhere in East Africa. Swahili was spread by trade from the east coastal areas in the precolonial period. It was fostered by the Germans and the English in the colonial period through official use and because it was employed as a medium of instruction in the schools in a highly multilingual area. Since independence came to Tanzania and Kenya, it has become an official language there, not only for convenience but as a symbol of nationhood and of African identity. Yet during this post-independence period it has acquired very few new first-language speakers. The many other languages of Africa continue to be spoken and are important vehicles of ethnic identity on the tribal level.

When a language spreads widely as an auxiliary language, many speakers will learn it from others for whom it is only a second language. There is a tendency in such instances for it to undergo often drastic grammatical simplification. Moreover, those who acquire it as a second language under such circumstances will superpose the sound system of their first language. It will, therefore, tend to differ in pronunciation according to the first languages of the speakers.

Such a form of a language with highly simplified grammar and nonstandardized pronunciation is called a "pidgin," (a corruption of the English word *business* originating in China). In the Katanga region of Zaïre, far from its original homeland, Swahili is spoken in such a pidginized form that it has a separate name, "Kingwana."

However, a language may be pidginized even when it is not primarily used as an auxiliary language between speakers

of different first languages. For example, the numerous
foreign workers in present-day West Germany, the so-called
Gastarbeiter 'guest workers', speak a pidginized form of
German, not so much as an auxiliary language with other
non-Germans, e.g., between Italian and Turk "guest workers,"
but when communicating with Germans. This pidginized German apparently resulted from the use of a simplified form of
German by the Germans themselves in talking with foreigners. Such "foreigner" talk is known to exist in many
areas and is highly conventionalized. For example, it almost
always uses only a single form of the verb, the infinitive, and
indicates person by independent pronouns instead of verb
inflections. Thus Italians in talking to foreigners will say *io
andare*, literally "I to-go," instead of the standard *vado*, 'I go'.

Similar origins are suggested for the pidginized forms of
English, French, and Portuguese that were used in the slave
trade and among slaves of different African language backgrounds in the New World. Highly pidginized forms of
English were also used in the Pacific islands and in China.

Sometimes pidginized languages reach a further stage and
become the first languages of speakers who no longer know
their ancestral languages. Such a form is called a "creole
language." An instance is Haitian Creole, the basic spoken
language of Haiti, which derives from the pidginized French
used in the slave trade. Such a language, once it has first-
language speakers, tends toward a standardized pronunciation
and begins to acquire the grammatical complications of non-
pidgin languages. It may then come under the influence of
the standard language of which it is a pidginized form and
borrow vocabulary from it. In Haiti, Creole exists alongside
standard French in a typical diglossia situation. Creole
speakers in varying degrees approximate and imitate the
standard form, depending on social status and education.

Language is not only a practical means of communication
but also an important and basic source of group identification. Even speakers with equal command of more than one
language have a different emotional attitude toward each.
Often one is the language of group affiliation, while the other
or others have more utilitarian functions and do not evoke

the same warm emotional feelings nor serve to the same degree as sources of solidarity with others who speak it.

Language, like all things which distinguish groups, is two-sided. On the one hand, it enhances the group feelings of those who share it, and on the other, it promotes a sense of difference from those with foreign modes of speech by setting the group apart as a distinctive entity.

Whether or not two forms of a language will become badges of group differences is a complex matter and depends not only on linguistic but also on social and political factors. Languages that are so different that mutual intelligibility is impossible are no doubt always vehicles for a sentiment of group distinctness, as, for example, Chinese and English in San Francisco. However, within the very wide range of difference in which mutual intelligibility is possible, feelings of linguistic distinctness may arise or not for essentially non-linguistic—for example, political—reasons. In certain circumstances wide differences may be overlooked, while in other cases relatively minute differences become a source of separate group identification.

Further, group identity is not itself a simple matter. The speaker of a local dialect may look on it as a distinguishing mark in relation to other local dialects. He may also be very well aware that in spite of these differences, there is common ground for affiliation at a higher level when in contrast to speakers of very different languages. For example, in ancient Greece, people had a powerful and primary loyalty to their own city, a loyalty largely symbolized by its distinct dialect. They also felt themselves to be Greek, on the basis of common language, against the barbarians, the common name assigned to all people whose first language was not Greek.

Indeed, the very notion of what is meant by a "distinct" language in common usage, depends not only on linguistic but also social and political factors. The linguist defines a language as a set of speech forms (dialects) among which mutual intelligibility exists. Language, however, as a sociolinguistic fact is not necessarily defined on this basis. For example, the local dialects of German differ greatly. The differences between extreme varieties are as great as those upon which a linguist studying local forms of speech in New Guinea would distinguish separate languages. Yet in Germany their speakers all consider them to be dialects of a single language, German. Further, a classification of these dialects on a purely linguistic basis would include local forms of Germanic spoken in Holland and Belgium as variants of a North German group of dialects (Low German). However, the speakers of these dialects in Holland and Belgium consider them to be variants of a different language, Dutch, because of political factors.

When speakers are asked to characterize the differences between their own speech and other very similar forms, most of these differences cannot be verbalized. After all, few of us are ever conscious of the structural facts about our own language. Vocabulary differences are the most easily noticed, while phonological differences are lumped together under "accent," though certain conspicuous sound differences may be conceptualized.

The important and pioneering work of William Labov on current sound change in certain populations speaking American English, shows that variant pronunciation of the same phoneme, even when not in the conscious awareness of speakers, become symbols of group identity.[3] For example, a study of the extent of the glides (i.e., tongue movements) in certain diphthongs, e.g., the *i* sound of words like *side*, showed that the extent of the glide among the native inhabitants of the island of Martha's Vineyard corresponded to the extent of commitment to the values of "islanders" as against those of the summer visitors and the outside world in general.

Up to now we have been considering sociolinguistic processes as they have developed spontaneously and without the intervention of conscious planning and decision making. However, language frequently does become the object of overtly articulated policies. There are at least three, often interconnected, aspects of explicit action in relation to lan-

[3] For a general account of this work, see William Labov, *Sociolinguistic Patterns* (Philadelphia: University of Pennsylvania Press, 1973).

guage: standardization, modernization, and the establishment of official languages.

Standardization is the development of a new uniform form of language which transcends the differences among the existing dialects. Linguistically, it is usually based on one particular dialect which already has attained some superiority on nonlinguistic grounds. Sometimes, however, a conscious attempt is made to develop a new form which incorporates widespread features of a number of different dialects.

Sometimes this may be based on a dialect survey and represent a "scientific" attempt in which linguistics are involved, but it may often be the result of more idiosyncratic individual activity. For example, in nineteenth-century Norway a man named Ivor Aasen literally invented a form of Norwegian which incorporated many widespread dialect features but which in its totality was not identical with any single dialect. It was widely adopted and became the basis of one of the two main standardized forms of Norwegian.

Standardization normally involves the introduction of a written norm where it did not exist and the publication of grammars and dictionaries intended to produce a single standard for the use of the language. However, standardization can occur even in a society without writing. The Homeric epics were composed in a supradialectal form of Greek which did not represent anyone's spoken dialect and existed even before the use of writing in Greece.

Today we may distinguish between standardized languages, which are used for traditional and limited purposes, and those that have the vocabulary required for instruction in higher education and scientific publication. The process of acquiring this vocabulary may be called "modernization."

In some instances, where the desire is to accomplish this rapidly, official language boards and academies are organized to develop systematically new vocabularies in scientific areas. Examples of this are Indonesia and Israel in which official bodies promulgate decisions in these matters which must then be implemented by teachers and writers of textbooks.

Language standardization and even modernization have sometimes in the past been undertaken by organizations other than government, e.g., missions and nationalistically oriented cultural societies. However, something further is involved when a language receives official governmental status. It then becomes the vehicle of a stated policy designed to foster a particular language as the expression of national unity, as in the case of the officially sanctioned Indonesian. At other times, it may receive a kind of subordinate or regional official status as the vehicle of ethnicity below the national level, as with Welsh in Wales.

Sociologists, in particular, have assumed that the world-wide spread of economic development, with its increased urbanization and world-wide economic and cultural interrelations, must lead to the decrease in the number of distinct languages and ultimately result in a single world language. However, recent experience has shown, on the one hand, the remarkable survival power of local languages as vehicles of ethnic and national identity and, on the other, the spread of international languages like English to satisfy the practical needs of communication foreseen by social scientists. People will continue to use more than one language especially where one is a means of expressing group solidarity and the other satisfies practical requirements of wider communication. In the past, multilingualism has been the rule rather than the exception. This situation is likely to continue in the foreseeable future.

Chapter 9

LANGUAGE AND HISTORY

We think of the historian's first task as constructing a true narrative of past events. But a more important task may be not only the re-creation of the events themselves but also a search for their causes. It is also often believed that history should investigate only the "important" political and military events, which appear to exercise a decisive influence in human affairs. But those historians who have thought most profoundly about their craft have recognized that the development of humanity's knowledge, the control of the environment or artistic creativity—in fact, any aspect of culture—deserve historical study. Historians traditionally have turned to written documents. But they need not confine themselves to these. After all, archaeologists deduce past events from materials much older than written records, and their pursuit is equally historical.

In addition to archaeology, what might be called "immaterial remains," neither documentary nor concrete in form, can test results attained by more conventional methods and supplement or even give rise to conclusions not attainable in other ways. One example is resemblance in customs, religious ceremonies, etc., as evidence of cultural contact. Among such immaterial sources, language in its historical aspect is the most important in the extent and accuracy of the conclusions it can provide.

In order to deduce nonlinguistic historical fact from language, we must apply the method of comparative history of which such results are important by-products.

All languages are constantly in the process of change, and these changes take different forms in the various localities in which a single language is spoken. As such "dialects" diverge they may eventually reach a point at which mutual intelligibility no longer exists, and they become separate but related languages. This process is a branching out of the original uniform language into a number of new languages, which form a "family." The metaphor commonly used is that of a genealogy and, just as human genealogies are described in terms of a family tree, so languages and their relationships can also be visualized and diagrammed in the same way. But this is a "one-sex" genealogy. Languages are, in this sense, personified as females. A language from which other languages descend is said to be their "mother language" and they are "sisters" to each other. There is nothing that corresponds to marriage since languages do not merge.

A classification of languages that reflects this branching is called a "genetic classification." How can such a classification be carried out? Where the languages have been written over a long period, the "mother" language from which the daughters descend may itself have been a literary language and so the whole process can be largely traced from written records. The best known example is the Romance languages, such as French, Italian, Spanish, Portuguese, and Romanian, all of which arose originally from various locally differentiated dialects of Latin.

But even if Latin had left no records, cursory examination of the languages of Europe as shown in the accompanying figure of common words would show that the Romance languages, because of their common origin, still greatly resemble each other. This becomes even more obvious when we compare them to non-Romance languages whose differences from the Romance languages immediately highlight the unity of this latter group.

Similarly we may note other groups of languages in Figure 9. For example, English, Dutch, German, Danish, Norwegian, Swedish, and Icelandic form another group, the Germanic languages. In this instance, however, the ancestral language which would correspond to Latin for the Romance

	two	three	head	eye	hand
IRISH	dó	trí	ceann	suil	lámh
WELSH	dau	tri	pen	llygad	llaw
ENGLISH	two	three	head	eye	hand
DUTCH	twee	drie	hoofd	oog	hand
GERMAN	zwei	drei	Kopf	Auge	Hand
DANISH	to	tre	hoved	øje	hånd
SWEDISH	två	tre	huvud	öga	hand
ICELANDIC	tveir	þrír	höfuð	auga	hönd
FRENCH	deux	trois	tête	oeil	main
ITALIAN	due	tre	testa	occhio	mano
SPANISH	dos	tres	cabeza	ojo	mano
ROMANIAN	doi	trei	cap	ochi	mînă
ALBANIAN	dy	tre	kryë	sy	dorë
GREEK	dhío	trís	kefáli	máti	khéri
LITHUANIAN	du	trys	galva	akis	ranka
LATVIAN	divi	trīs	galva	acs	roka
RUSSIAN	dva	tri	golova	glaz	ruka
POLISH	dwa	trzy	głowa	oko	ręka
CZECH	dva	tři	hlava	oko	ruka
SERBO-CROATIAN	dva	tri	glava	oko	ruka
FINNISH	kaksi	kolme	pää	silmä	käsi
ESTHONIAN	kaks	kolm	pea	silm	käsi
HUNGARIAN	két	három	fej	szem	kéz
BASQUE	bi	iru	buru	begi	esku

Figure 9.

group has left no written records because at the time and in the area where it was spoken, writing did not exist. In such instances, and such will usually be the case, we speak of a "protolanguage," in this instance, Proto-Germanic.

Since we lack direct documentation for Proto-Germanic the question arises whether we can discover anything of a concrete or detailed nature regarding this language. This is precisely where we would use the comparative method of reconstruction. Given our knowledge of the process of linguistic change and a systematic comparison of the descendant languages, i.e., the contemporary Germanic languages, we can work backwards and postulate in considerable detail and with a large degree of confidence many linguistic features of Proto-Germanic, such as its basic sound system, grammatical structure, and vocabulary.

Even where, as in the case of Latin, we have direct documentation, it is, of course, possible to apply the same comparative method, and in fact this has been done. Interestingly, the reconstructed Proto-Romance language is not precisely like literary Latin. Called "vulgar Latin," it was presumably the actual spoken language of the early Roman Empire. Occasional misspelling in inscriptions shows us that our reconstructed vulgar Latin was in fact essentially identical with this spoken form of Latin.

It is often possible to penetrate still further back in time to groupings more fundamental than "Romance" or "Germanic." After all, Latin, Proto-Germanic, and, we may add, Proto-Slavic, Ancient Greek, and others were languages like those of the present day but simply spoken at an earlier period. Comparing these in turn indicates still deeper groupings and suggests successive branchings at different time periods.

The larger grouping to which most of the languages of Europe and many in Western Asia and into Northern India belong is called "Indo-European." Just as English, German, Dutch, etc., arose from dialect splits in an earlier language, Proto-Germanic, so in turn Proto-Germanic, Proto-Slavic, Proto-Indic, etc., were originally dialects of a still earlier language which has left no written records. This language is known as Proto-Indo-European and for more than a century many scholars have been reconstructing in considerable detail its linguistic features by comparing the various subfamilies of Indo-European languages.

Not all languages of Europe or the Middle East are Indo-European, of course. For example, in Europe, Finnish and Esthonian, closely related to each other, are non-Indo-

European languages and related distantly to Hungarian. All three are part of a large subfamily whose other members are spoken in parts of the Soviet Union and Siberia and is known as Finno-Ugric. Similarly, there are other languages elsewhere which belong to still other families.

We need to be acquainted with one additional basic concept before we can begin to consider some of the linguistic methods that can be used for historical purpose. This is the notion of cognate forms. When languages belong to the same family, they often keep in altered form the original form which was part of the ancestral or protolanguage. Such related forms are known as "cognates." Thus English *three* and French *trois* (pronounced /trwa/) are cognates since they both are independent continuations of the early Indo-European form of the English word *three*, which is reconstructed as having the root *trei-*. Such cognates, which are the varying resultants of a single form in the protolanguage are to be distinguished from another kind of resemblance which results from borrowing or later contact as in the English word *garage*, which is borrowed from French, or the French word *sport*, which is borrowed from English. Languages can, of course, borrow terms both from related and unrelated languages. The methods of comparative linguistics, even in the absence of written records, often permit us to distinguish between these two sources of resemblances among languages, which is as important as their implications for historical knowledge are different.

By the comparison of cognate forms in related languages, it becomes possible to reconstruct sequences of sounds with their meanings in the protolanguage as was noted above in the case of Proto-Indo-European, e.g., *trei-*, *three*. The totality of such reconstructed words makes up what we call the "protovocabulary," which is the basis for one major source of the historical knowledge linguistics provides.

Clearly some of the words will tell us nothing of cultural significance. For example, we can reconstruct a Proto-Indo-European word for "nose." That the Proto-Indo-European speech community had a word for "nose" is hardly surprising and is of no historical significance. However, other parts of the vocabulary are of considerable historical interest. A whole series of words can be reconstructed that show that the Indo-European speakers had a typical Neolithic (New Stone Age) village economy based on the practice of mixed farming involving certain domesticated animals and plants and the use of the plow, that they were also acquainted with the horse and perhaps had already begun to use it as a riding animal. Among the words that can be reconstructed are those for *cultivated field, plow, cow, goat, goose, duck, horse, grain,* and *barley*.

On the other hand, as Buck, author of a work on Proto-Indo-European vocabulary, notes "the use of iron is comparatively late in history, long after the Indo-European unity. Most of the words [for iron] are of obscure origin."[1]

Beyond information regarding a New Stone Age economy, it is possible to reconstruct from other words a good part of its kinship system and even of its religion, because the names of some divinities are reconstructible and there are some agreements in the myths told about them among the earliest Indo-European peoples.

It is sometimes possible to show borrowings involving one or more protolanguages. For example, Finnish has a number of words of obvious Germanic origin. The phonetic form they take in Finnish, however, does not reflect any specific present-day Germanic language but rather Proto-Germanic as reconstructed by linguists from the comparative study of the Germanic languages. The types of words involved and the fact that there are apparently no loan words in the opposite direction shows that at this early period the speakers of Proto-Germanic and early Finnish must have been in geographical contact and that it was the former who influenced the latter culturally.

How does the sort of information revealed by comparative linguistics on the cultural characteristics of the speakers of the Proto-Indo-European language relate to archaeological inquiry? Can we identify the speakers of this language with a

[1] Carl Darling Buck, *A Dictionary of Selected Synonyms in the Principal Indo-European Languages* (Chicago: Chicago University Press, 1949), p. 613.

particular culture known from its archaeological remains? So far the archaeologist will have a fairly detailed notion of the kind of culture he will be dealing with and hence the sorts of material remains he expects it will have left. However, two crucial questions regarding the speakers of Proto-Indo-European remain unanswered: where and when they lived. Regarding their place of origin, there are two main lines of reasoning. The first refers to the existence of reconstructible vocabulary that will tell us something about the sort of geographical environment in which this ancestral people lived. Original words for particular wild plants and animals, the existence of a word for "ocean," "snow," etc., are examples of the kind of data which are important here. For Indo-European, two terms have played a special role, *beech tree* and *salmon*, and these have helped to fix an approximate area of origin somewhere between the Crimea and the northern Caucasus. The second involves the present and past locations of speakers of the separate languages that descended from earlier dialects of the same protolanguage. The place of origin of the protolanguage ought to be reasonably central in relation to later distributions. For example, the Indo-European speakers are now distributed over a vast area, from the Celtic region in the extreme west of Europe (Brittany, Wales, Ireland) to the Aryan region which covers Iran and northern India, most of Pakistan, and Bangladesh. To place the origin of Indo-European in India at one extreme end of the distribution is highly improbable. It would mean that by some conspiracy all the speakers of the other dialects of the protolanguage had decided to migrate westward. An analogous argument will, of course, rule out Ireland in the extreme west.

This sort of reasoning has developed into a more exact theory which is called the "theory of least moves" or the "center of gravity theory." A distribution in which just one subgroup is far removed from all the rest—the theory of least moves—obviously indicates that it was the one that moved and not all the rest. A striking example may be found in Africa where a particular set of linguistic facts and its explanation have become the focal point for the archaeology that deals with the last 3,000 years of African history.

Almost all of South, East, and Central Africa are inhabited by peoples who speak languages of the Bantu family. There are several hundred of these languages. Among the best known are Swahili in East Africa, Zulu in South Africa, and Kikongo in Zaïre.

The Bantu languages are not much more different from each other than Romance languages are from each other, and these degrees of similarity contrast with the great disparities among languages spoken across Africa in the area farther north—the Guinea Coast of West Africa and the interior area known as the Sudan.

All this suggests that Proto-Bantu must have been spoken relatively recently since there has not been time for great differences to develop among its component languages. Further, if it is recent, it should not be difficult to establish that it is only a branch of some much larger family. In fact, this can be shown to be true. Proto-Bantu is but one of the vast assemblage of languages called Niger-Congo, which centers geographically in West Africa. Moreover, Proto-Bantu belongs to a particular branch of that family called Benue-Congo. All of the non-Bantu languages in the Benue-Congo branch are found in that part of Nigeria immediately to the northwest of the present Bantu area. Within the Benue-Congo branch, Bantu is most closely related to a small group of languages in eastern Nigeria.

The conclusion to be drawn from this is that Bantu speakers must have spread in relatively recent times from an area immediately to the northwest of their present area and settled vast areas of East, Central, and South Africa. This is known because the Bantu migration and its study have become the main topic of archaeological investigation in the recent period in Africa.

Whom did the Bantu speakers displace over this vast area? Again linguistics gives us part of the answer. Speakers of the so-called Khoisan languages, mainly the Bushmen and Hottentots of South Africa, are still living there. Moreover, two languages only distantly related to the South African languages and very different from each other are spoken by populations much farther to the north in East Africa. These are the Sandawe and Hatsa of Tanzania.

This linguistic stock must be very old in East and South Africa. The archaeological remains left by their speakers, who were nonagricultural, are characteristically different from those of the incoming Bantu.

Naturally, there are complications to the somewhat simple picture presented here. In the present context, however, what we wish to show is that facts about relationships of languages provide the main hypotheses that have guided archaeological research in regard to the last several thousand years of African history.

But how long ago was Proto-Indo-European spoken by a relatively unified speech community? When did it begin to break up into separate and mutually unintelligible languages which came to form the different branches of the family?

Glottochronology provides us with an educated guess regarding the date when the protolanguage of any family of languages began to diverge. The basic idea behind glottochronology is that the greater the age of a linguistic family, the longer the individual languages have been diverging and the less their resemblance. But how can this degree of resemblance be measured? How can we assign an absolute date in years to the period of divergence rather than merely a relative one as between one family and another?

The aspect of language used for measurement is what is called "basic vocabulary." There is a standard list of over two hundred items and a shorter, more convenient one of one hundred items which is more frequently employed. The basic vocabulary includes such items as low numerals, e.g., *one, two;* the pronouns *I, you, we;* words for parts of the human body such as *eye, hand, nose;* common actions like *eat, sleep;* and fundamental and universal aspects of the human environment such as *fire, water,* etc. Such items are part of the vocabulary of all known languages and persist over long periods— i.e., they are not often replaced by new terms.

Let us suppose we are dealing with two sets of unrelated languages but each set contains two languages that are related to each other. Suppose that the languages of the first set, A and B, began to diverge from each other a very long time ago, while those of the second set, C and D, began to diverge very recently. Then we may expect that of the original one hundred words, many more would have been replaced in A and B than in C and D. Whenever two words for the same basic item, e.g., water, have not been replaced in either of the two languages, they will of course be continuing the same original form and be cognates. Hence we may expect that for A and B, which are hypothesized to be only distantly related, the percentage of such cognates on our one-hundred word list will be much smaller than for the pair of languages C and D, which have only recently differentiated from each other. The proportion of cognates on our fixed list will provide a kind of measure of the relative degree of divergence and hence the age of one language family compared to another.

Without going into the mathematics involved, one will clearly now have a relative measure of degree of divergence.[2] The question arises whether we can say only, for example, that the ancestral language of A and B is five times older than that of C and D, or whether it is also possible to give an absolute chronology specifying the number of years.

If we assume that each item on the list is independent of all the others and that all languages will replace them at approximately the same rate, then our question will take the following form: What proportion of the original list will be replaced within a given time period, say one thousand years?

We can take languages that have persisted in written form over long periods of time, e.g., Ancient Greek and Modern Greek, Latin and French, the earliest Babylonian and the latest before being replaced by Aramaic (a period of at least two thousand years), and investigate the specific list of one hundred (or the longer list), noting what proportion of the original list has been replaced over a millenium. In doing this, we find that of the hundred-word list, approximately twenty items will be replaced over a period of a thousand years.

Then two languages that have been separated for a thou-

---

[2] For a clear mathematical exposition, see Sarah C. Gudschinsky, "The ABCs of Lexicostatics (Glottochronology)," *Word* 12 (1956), 175–210.

sand years should each retain 80 per cent of the words on the list. If the 80 per cent retained is in each case randomly drawn from the list and independent, the percentage of cognate words between the two languages will be $.80 \times .80 = .64$.

There are a number of difficulties inherent in the above procedures. The most important is probably that the hundred words are not all equally stable. Hence in the first thousand years it will be the least stable words that will be lost. Hence the loss is *not* random, and short dates will be overestimated and long dates underestimated. The method, however, still gives results which are of interest but should, of course, not be taken too literally.

Such data are, of course, important in correlating archaeological with linguistic evidence since archaeology, beginning with the inception of the carbon-14 method of dating artifacts shortly after World War II, has developed a whole series of devices which provide absolute chronologies.

A further method for studying history through language is the study of words borrowed between peoples who have been in contact with each other over an extended period. When resemblances are attributed to borrowing, historical linguistics can usually tell us which language was the source language and which the borrowing language.

It is also often possible, from the kinds and extent of phonetic changes to say something about the relative dates of borrowing. Sometimes words fall into several chronological strata. The meanings of the words are, of course, valuable clues to the nature of the cultural influences in various periods.

As one example of the study of loan words, let us look at the Hausa people in northern Nigeria in West Africa. From historical documents we think the Hausa became Moslems in the fifteenth century. There are numerous loan words from Arabic in the Hausa language. These fall into two chronological strata: an early group where the words themselves indicate the borrowing of such cultural traits as writing and various terms having to do with the riding of horses (such words as those for *saddle, bridle,* etc.); and a more recent group where terms refer to more specifically religious and learned terminology drawn from literary Arabic.

A further type of historical study is one in which we are interested in the spread of a particular complex of cultural traits, for example, the use of iron. Here we can enrich the historical picture by studying the distribution of terminology of ironworking in different languages to discover how these words have spread by borrowing from language to language. We can combine this with the historical-comparative method. For example, if we can determine that these words existed in an ancestor language of a present grouping, then we know that ironworking is at least as old in this area as the time this language was spoken.

Altogether, the basic methods outlined here constitute a rich arsenal, which, together with other types of historical evidence, tells us much about the human past that would otherwise be lost. In many parts of the world where written evidence is only available for the quite recent past, people seek to know and understand their own historical roots and to this endeavor linguistic methods can make a worthy contribution.

Chapter 10

PSYCHOLINGUISTICS

Psycholinguistics—which combines linguistics and psychology—is one of today's most vigorous interdisciplinary areas. Most often it is the linguist who comes forward with the questions to be tested, while the psychologist provides the psychological interpretations and the experimental techniques.

For partly historical reasons, most psycholinguists belong to psychology departments. The psychology of language has been a branch of psychology as far back as the nineteenth century. So when recent developments in linguistics, particularly the rise of transformational theory, began to direct the attention of psychologists to current linguistics, there was already a well-established tradition in psychology for this kind of study which was lacking in linguistics. The only area in which this was not true was in the study of the child's acquisition of language, where, if either, linguists have predominated.

We will now turn to several concrete psycholinguistic investigations in order to give something of the flavor of the field. The first study concerns phonology and is based on some of the work the author, a linguist, carried out in collaboration with James Jenkins, a psychologist whose specialty is the psychology of language.[1]

The question we investigated was a specific problem among the many which had to do with the "psychological reality" of linguistic analyses.

[1] "Studies in the Psychological Correlates of the Sound System of American English I," *Word* 20 (1964), 157–77.

In the earlier treatment of phonological systems in Chapter 3 we noted that speech sounds have distinctive features. For example, the *b* sound of English is voiced as opposed to *p;* it is also nonnasal in contrast to *m;* and it is bilabial unlike *d*, which is alveolar (tip of the tongue against the alveolar ridge behind the teeth) in its point of articulation; finally, *b* is a stop sound as opposed to fricative continuants like *v*.

When we define sounds in terms of distinctive features we are also ordering them in terms of psychological similarity. For example, if two sounds such as *b* and *p* differ in only one distinctive feature, namely, voicing versus nonvoicing, they should seem more similar to each other than, say, *b* and *k* since *b* differs from *k* not only in voicing but also in point of articulation (both *b* and *p* being bilabial and *k* being velar).

Where two pairs of sounds are distinguished by the same set of contrastive features, each pair should be judged about equally similar. For example, the phonetic proportion $p:b=k:g$ (where for each pair the first member is identical to the second except for absence of voicing in the first member and its presence in the second) should produce the psychological judgment that *p* is about as similar to *b* as *k* is to *g*.

To test hypotheses of this sort, we chose six English consonants[2] whose patterning based on distinctive features is represented below:

	Bilabial	Alveolar	Velar
Unvoiced	*p*	*t*	*k*
Voiced	*b*	*d*	*g*

Figure 10.

The *g* referred to is, of course, that found in the word *get*, not that in *gin*.

[2] One reason for choosing only six sounds is that each additional sound means a continually increasing increment to the number of sets of pairs presented to the person being tested. Since each pair has to be presented in both orders to take into account possible order effects, with six consonants each subject is presented with thirty sets of stimuli. For example, *b* is followed by *t; t* is followed by *b; k* is followed by *g; g* is followed by *k;* etc.

What we were looking for was a measurement of psycho-logical distance between each of these consonants. We could then try to construct a "psychological space" and see how it related to that implied in the figure above.

There were four separate experiments, each involving five people. The experiments will be called A, B, C, and D. In experiment A the pairs of stimuli were presented both visu-ally and orally. Each consonant was followed by a dummy vowel *a* (pronounced as in *father*). Each person had a sheet of paper with thirty pairs of consonants followed by a blank space:

1. *pa*   *ba*   _____
2. *pa*   *ga*   _____
3. *etc.*

On a recorded tape each pair was pronounced in order and each person wrote a number in the blank. Any number might be chosen for the first blank. Let us say that it was 10. This was to represent an estimate of how different the two conso-nants were. If it was felt that the second pair was much less similar, say three times less, that person might write 30. If they seemed more similar, it might be 5. Each person could thus develop an individual scale. There were two trial runs to allow the subject to work out a scale and get used to the task. Only the results of the third trial were used. Experi-ment B was of the same design as A except that there was only oral, not visual presentation. Experiment C was simply a repetition of B in order to obtain a larger sample in view of the variability of the results up to that point.

The method just described is called "free-magnitude estima-tion." It was then a new technique and one of the purposes of these experiments was to test its validity. We did this in Experiment D which used the standard method of a rating scale. The stimuli for D were oral only, as they were for B and C.

The instruction sheet for Experiment D had the following appearance:

1. :   :   :   :   :   :

extremely	decidedly	pretty	somewhat	slightly	not
similar	similar	similar	similar	similar	similar

2. :   :   :   :   :   :

extremely	decidedly	pretty	somewhat	slightly	not
similar	similar	similar	similar	similar	similar

As with the previous experiments, each person was presented with pairs such as *ba* and *da,* but this time their similarity was judged by circling the colon above the appropriate similarity rating.

We evaluated the results of these experiments in the following way.

First, we made the different magnitude-estimation scales of the people in Experiments A, B, and C and the rating scale in Experiment D comparable by putting them into rank order.

For each pair of syllables differing in order only, for example, *pa–ta* and *ta–pa,* the raw scores were averaged to get a single measure of distance. The fifteen different scores obtained were then ordered, the smallest, which of course represented the greatest similarity, assigned the number 1, the largest 15. Then these ranks were averaged across the twenty subjects in all four experiments. The results are shown in the following table in which the pairs of consonants are ranked in order of judgments of closeness.

TABLE I

	Average Ranks	Rank Order
bd	3.225	1
gd	4.750	2
pb	5.850	3
kg	6.075	4
bg	6.550	5
pt	6.575	6
kt	7.575	7
td	8.000	8
pd	9.975	9

pk	10.025	10
tb	10.150	11
tc	10.250	12
kd	10.275	13
kb	10.350	14
pg	10.600	15

Measures summarizing the relative importance of agreements and disagreements in particular features were easily obtained by averaging the foregoing results. For example, for the feature of point of articulation, by taking the pairs which are at the same point of articulation, i.e., *pb*, *td*, and *kg*, and averaging their distance, we obtained a general measure of the importance of agreement in this feature. Thus we add 5.850 (*pb*), 8.000 (*td*), and 6.075 (*kg*) and divide by 3 to arrive at 6.642, the third entry in Table II below. The table gives the results of such averaging agreement for features of voicing and point of articulation, for differences between each pair of points of articulation, and for agreement in one feature as against agreement in two features. A larger number, of course, indicates a judgment of greater psychological distance.

TABLE II

1.	agreement in possession of voicing	4.825
2.	agreement in non-voicing	8.042
3.	agreement in point of articulation	6.642
4.	alveolar-labial contrast	7.325
5.	alveolar-velar contrast	8.187
6.	labial-velar contrast	9.356
7.	difference in one feature	6.503
8.	difference in two features	10.146

The difference between the seventh and eighth items shows that, in general, feature analysis is consistent with judgments of sound similarity. Pairs of sounds which agree in all but one feature are judged as substantially more similar than those with a two-feature difference, 6.503 as against 10.146.

Secondly, distances between points of articulation are ranked as follows: labial-alveolar, alveolar-velar, and labial-velar. This ranking corresponds rather closely to articulatory facts. The tip of the tongue in the alveolar articulation of *t* and *d* is close to the lips which are involved in the bilabial stops *b* and *d*. The distance between the alveolar closure and the velar closure against soft palate at the back of the mouth is greater. The greatest distance of all is, of course, between labials and velars.

The third result could not have been predicted by simply weighting each feature equally. From a comparison of the figures in the first two lines of Table II, we see that agreement in voicing counts more heavily in leading to judgments of similarity than agreement in nonvoicing, e.g., *b* and *d* are judged to be much closer to each other than the corresponding pairs *p* and *t*.

This, at first surprising, result fits in very well with the theory of marking described earlier. Voicing is the marked feature. Phonetically it represents an added something, namely, vibration of the vocal chords, which when present in two otherwise dissimilar sounds makes them more similar. On the other hand, the unmarked feature of voicelessness is the absence of this vibration, and as such it does not increase perceived similarity.

Figure 11 schematically diagrams the psychological space of the six consonants resulting from this set of experiments.

These observations about marked features are related to other facts. For example, in regard to historical change, voiced sounds, being more similar to each other, are less likely to be kept apart perceptually and therefore to merge in the course of sound change.

The second set of experiments is similar to those just discussed in that it also concerns the problem of the psychological reality of linguistic units. However, the units being investigated are on the grammatical rather than the phonological level, and the experimental technique used is a very different one. The study was carried out in 1965 by two psycholinguists, J. A. Fodor and T. G. Bever, both originally psychologists rather than linguists, but with a linguistic sophistication characteristic of the more recent generation of psychologists.

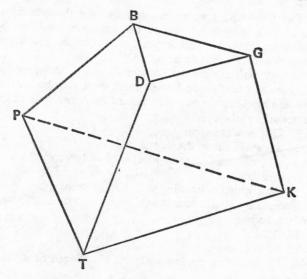

Figure 11.

Their results are presented in an article entitled "The Psychological Reality of Linguistic Segments."[3]

The central concept in syntactical analysis developed by structuralists was immediate-constituent analysis. A sentence was viewed as a hierarchical organization in which certain elements were more closely related to each other to form constituent structures and these lower-level structures in turn were entered as unit constituents at higher levels up to the sentence as the highest level. Although in transformational theory these relationships were viewed as surface phenomena resulting from transformations of deeper structures often very differently organized, such analysis into constituents was viewed as valid and one which might therefore be tested in regard to its psychological correlates in the behavior of speakers of the language.

[3] J. A. Fodor and T. G. Bever, "The Psychological Reality of Linguistic Segments," *Journal of Verbal Learning and Verbal Behavior* 4 (1966), 30–32.

For illustrative purposes we may consider the immediate-constituent analysis of one of the sentences employed by Fodor and Bever in their experiment: "That he was happy was evident from the way he smiled."

If we start from the top down, the main break within the sentence is after "happy," after which there may be a pause in speaking. Thus the two chief immediate constituents of the sentence as a whole are:

1. That he was happy
2. was evident from the way he smiled.

Each of these can in turn be analyzed into lower level immediate constituents.

Starting with the constituent 1, it may be analyzed as itself consisting of two constituents which we may call IA and IB, respectively.

IA–That
IB–he was happy.

Now IA cannot be further analyzed, but IB can be divided as follows:

IBa–he
IBb–was happy.

IBb can be further analyzed into

IBba–was
IBbb–happy

This type of analysis can be shown diagrammatically by the use of parentheses. If we take the first main constituent "That he was happy" as an example, the following diagram is an equivalent way of symbolizing the preceding analysis:

((That) ((he) ((was) (happy))))

The second main constituent "was evident from the way he smiled," can be analyzed in the same way.

This kind of constituent analysis provides a hierarchy of boundaries. In the above parenthesization, the more restrictive the boundary, the larger the number of parentheses. Thus, in a diagramming of the entire sentence, the largest number of parentheses will occur after *happy*, which is the boundary of a whole series of constituents at various levels and marks the most fundamental binary division within the sentence.

The experimental technique employed by Fodor and Bever

was one used in an earlier, similar experiment by Peter Ladefoged and D. E. Broadbent in 1960.[4] This experimental method is dichotic listening and is now being actively used in a whole series of studies with varied purposes. It is possible to feed through earphones different acoustic signals into the right and left ears of a subject simultaneously and have the subject report what he hears. The earlier Ladefoged and Broadbent study initiated a particular technique in dichotic listening. The stimulus to one ear consisted of meaningful material while that to the other consisted of bursts of noise (called "clicks") which were made to coincide with particular points of the meaningful material. In the Ladefoged-Broadbent experiment two types of meaningful material were used— strings of random digits and sentences. The former would presumably not be subject to any internal grouping or organization while the latter was organized grammatically and exhibited a total meaning structure. It was found that there was a statistically significant difference in accuracy of the location of the clicks when synchronized with these two types of material; it was far more accurate with sentences than with digits. It was as though the structuring of the sentence presented a more coherent reference background against which the clicks could be located.

The purpose of the Fodor-Bever experiment was to test whether this coherent structure correlated with the immediate-constituent analysis of the sort carried out by linguists. Thirty sentences were constructed of the same type as "That he was happy was evident from the way he smiled." Each sentence was complex in the sense that it had a single main constituent break like the one after *happy* in the sentence above.

Each of these sentences, after it was recorded, was re-recorded nine times on tape so that each rendition was identical. Then each of the nine copies was synchronized to a click in a different position which could be fed into one of the persons' ears while the sentence without the clicks was fed into

[4] P. Ladefoged and D. E. Broadbent, "Perception of Sequence in Auditory Events," *Quarterly Journal of Psychology* 13 (1960), 162–70.

the other. These nine clicks were located as follows. One was at the break between the main constituents (this is labeled "0" in the diagram below). Three labeled "+1," "+2," and "+3," respectively, were in the middle of the first, second, and third syllable following this break. Three more, labeled "−1," "−2," and "−3," were correspondingly placed in the middle of the three syllables which preceded the break. There were two more, labeled "a" and "b" in the accompanying diagram, so that a was placed at the word boundary one word before the main constituent boundary and b at the word boundary one word after the main boundary. The location of these clicks in the specimen sentence is illustrated in Figure 12.

```
                •                      •
... was    •  hap- py    was      •  e-    vi- dent ...
                •                      •
     −3    •  −2  −1   0   +1     •  +2  +3
                •                      •
                •                      •
                a                      b
```

Figure 12.

Each of the thirty sentences was recorded with the click in these nine different positions. The subjects were nine groups of four right-handed students each. The reason for choosing right-handed students is that left-handed and right-handed people process information differently through their right and left ears.

Each of the nine groups heard each of the thirty sentences with the click in one of the nine positions, different positions being used for different sentences. Each sentence had all of its nine copies distributed one each to the nine groups. Of the four members of each group, two had the sentence fed to the right ear and the click to the left, and the other two, the opposite.

The basic hypothesis of the experimenters was that "the units of speech perception correspond to the constituent." For this experiment, such units should resist interruption in the sense that clicks located within syllables should be perceived incorrectly more often and should be moved toward word boundaries, predominantly in the direction of the major break. For example, people should tend to hear a click placed at the +3 position earlier and closer to 0, which is the major constituent boundary of the sentence. Similarly, they should hear the −3 click later than the actual physical stimulus. Moreover, there should be fewest errors in perception of the click at the 0 position because it coincides with the main-constituent boundary of the sentence.

These hypotheses were borne out experimentally. Significantly more of the correctly located clicks were at the major break (0 position). The remainder were subject to 80 per cent error. Of these 66 per cent were in the predicted direction, i.e., toward the major boundary, and the remaining 34 per cent in the direction not predicted. These are highly significant results statistically.

As these two experiments are presented, it might appear that the results are in principle of greater interest to linguists than psychologists. But important psychological issues are involved.

The Greenberg-Jenkins experiment involved a question of psychological methodology (the free-magnitude estimation technique versus the better established rating-scale method), which is clearly of more interest to psychologists than to linguists. The Fodor-Bever experiment contrasted two classically different psychological theories of perception—the stimulus-response behaviorist theory, according to which the brain responds in terms of the physical properties of each stimulus as such, and the Gestalt view, according to which human beings perceive in terms of organized wholes.

Indeed, the results seem to favor the latter. The Fodor-Bever experiment had an aftermath in connection with this view. Their interpretation was criticized on the grounds that the people being tested might not be responding to the higher-level grammatical organization of the sentence but to the acoustic property of pause at the main constituent boundary. This led Fodor and Bever to re-examine their results. Full pauses occurred in eight of the recorded sentences, six showed severe drops in acoustic intensity at the boundary but not to zero, eight showed a mild drop in intensity, while four showed no measurable pause or intensity drop. The re-examination showed that there was no relation between the proportion or direction of errors based on this factor of acoustic pause.

This problem was investigated more fully in a later set of experiments by Garrett, Bever, and Fodor, which seemed definitely to rule out the purely acoustic factor.[5] In the words of the experimenters, "the primary significance of these results is the support they provide for a view of the sentence decoding as an active process in which the listener provides the structural analysis of the sentence rather than responding passively to some acoustic cue."

[5] M. F. Garrett, T. G. Bever, and J. A. Fodor, "The Active Use of Grammar in Speech Perception," *Perception and Psychophysics,* 1 (1966), 30–32.

Chapter 11

LANGUAGE DIVERSITY AND
LANGUAGE UNIFORMITY

To what extent are the thousands of diverse languages of the world similar and to what extent do they differ? Are there any fundamental similarities in all languages of the world? Well, linguistic determinism of the Whorfian type would certainly underscore the *differences* among languages, since it holds that every language embodies a particular and idiosyncratic world view. On the other hand, a discussion of fundamental features of all major aspects of language would suggest that beneath the undoubted and obvious dissimilarities among languages, there exist general principles common to all languages. This position has been expressed by Chomsky and the transformationalists, and the existence and nature of such common features has been a hot topic in recent linguistics. The term "language universal" has come to be applied to linguistic properties of this sort. Evidently we expect such principles, if they exist, to tell us something significant regarding the principles by which the human mind operates.

We will look at a single brief sentence in a small number of geographically and structurally diverse languages in order to see the ways in which languages typically resemble and differ from each other.

The sentence is: "The boy drank the water." The languages are English, Russian, Turkish, Classical Arabic, Hausa, Thai, and Quechua. (Hausa, as we have seen, is a language spoken widely in West Africa; Quechua was the language of the Incas and is still spoken by millions of people in western South America.)

The sentences in these seven languages may be rendered as follows:

1. English: the bóy dránk the wáter
2. Russian: mál'čik výpil vódu
3. Turkish: çocúk suyú içtí
4. Arabic: šáraba lwáladu lmáʔa
5. Hausa: yằrð yášá rúwắ
6. Thai: dègchaaj dỳym nàam
7. Quechua: wámbra yakúta upiárqan

Table III

	1	2 case	3 gender	4 number	5 definiteness	6 word order
1. English	the bóy	−	−	+	+	1
2. Russian	mál'čik	+	+	+	−	1
3. Turkish	çocúk	+	−	+	−	1
4. Arabic	l-wálad-u	+	+	+	+	2
5. Hausa	yằrð	−	+	+	−	1
6. Thai	dèg-chaaj	−	−	−	−	1
7. Quechua	wámbra	+	−	+	−	1

Table IV

	1	2 tense	3 completion	4 agreement with subject	5 word order
1. English	dránk	+	+	none	2
2. Russian	vý-p i-l	+	+	gender, number	2
3. Turkish	iç-tí	+	+	person, number	3
4. Arabic	šárab-a	+	+	gender, person, number	1
5. Hausa	yắ-šá	+	+	gender, person, number	2
6. Thai	dỳym	−	+	none	2
7. Quechua	upiá-rqa-n	+	+	person, number	3

Table V

	1	2 case	3 gender	4 number	5 definiteness	6 word order
1. English	the wáter	–	–	+	+	3
2. Russian	vód-u	+	+	+	–	3
3. Turkish	su-yú	+	–	+	+	2
4. Arabic	l-mâʔ-a	+	+	+	+	3
5. Hausa	rúwǎ	–	+	+	–	3
6. Thai	nàam	–	–	–	–	3
7. Quechua	yakú-ta	+	–	+	–	2

Since the discussion will mainly concern the grammatical structural rather than the phonology, explanations of the phonetic values of the symbols used are in the accompanying footnote.[1]

Analysis is facilitated by reference to Tables III, IV, and V, above, in which *the boy, drank,* and *the water,* respectively, are specified in relation to a number of categories in the seven languages.

Column 1 of each table contains the word or words in English and the six other languages. Hyphens indicate divi-

[1] In English, Russian, Turkish, Classical Arabic, and Quechua ′ indicates accentual prominence (the so-called stress accent). In Hausa ′ indicates a musically high pitch and ‵ a low pitch. In Thai, which is tonal like Hausa, the accent ‵ also indicates low pitch.

In Russian *č* is pronounced like *ch* in *cheese; l′* is a palatalized *l* with the simultaneous pronunciation of a *y* as in *yard.* The letter *y* indicates a vowel something like *u* but without the lips being rounded.

In Turkish *ç* is pronounced like *ch* in *cheese* and *c* like *j* in *jam.* In Arabic and Hausa *š* is like *sh* in *shell.* In Arabic *ʔ* is a glottal stop, i.e., a closing of the vocal chords with audible release. This sound is found in some speakers of English in words like *bottle* in place of *tt.*

In Hausa and Arabic lines over vowels indicate long vowels. In Thai *y* is pronounced approximately like the *y* described above for Russian. Double vowels indicate prolongation of the vowel sounds.

In Quechua *q* is a uvular stop pronounced by placing the back of the tongue against the uvula and releasing it explosively.

sions within the words. The pluses and minuses indicate the presence or absence of expression of a category. In Table III, containing the subject of the sentence, *the boy*, column 2 refers to the category of case. A plus here indicates that the grammatical form of the word refers to the subject, that is, the actor in the sentence. For example, in Quechua, if *the boy* had been the object of the action, the word would have been *wambrá-ta*, not *wámbra*, with the objective case indicated by the suffix *-ta*.

Column 3 in Table III refers to gender. Three of the languages, Russian, Arabic, and Hausa, have grammatical gender, as indicated by the plus sign. Russian has three (masculine, feminine, and neuter), while Arabic and Hausa each has two (masculine and feminine). The gender of a noun in these languages essentially requires gender agreement in affiliated words. Thus, if a noun is accompanied by an adjective in any of these languages, the adjective will take a form that agrees with the noun. In these three languages, gender is natural to the extent that masculine human beings are normally in the masculine gender while feminine human beings are normally in the feminine. However, for sexless entities the assignment is unpredictable. Thus *water* is feminine in Russian but masculine in Arabic and Hausa. For animals the most common treatment in languages with sex gender is for some species as a whole to be grammatically masculine and some to be grammatically feminine. Occasionally, especially for domesticated species, they will be differentiated with grammatically masculine terms for the male, and feminine for the female. However, many languages of the world divide nouns into gender classes without biological sex being among the criteria for classification. In such systems, humanness or animacy in general always figures among the criteria for assignment to a class.

Column 4 in Table III refers to number. In all of the seven languages except Thai it is possible to tell from the form of the noun whether it is one or many boys who are involved. In Thai *dèg-chaaj* could be one or more than one boy; however, if it became necessary in Thai to specify singular, the word for *one* would be used. Where number can be determined from the context, it is not expressed in Thai. Classical Arabic differs from the other languages in the table in that it has three number categories—singular, plural, and dual, which is employed when there are two members of the class being referred to. Thus, in Classical Arabic *waladāni* would be used for *two boys* and *?awlād* for more than two.

Column 5 in Table III refers to definiteness, i.e., whether a noun is assumed to be identified from previous mention or the general context (indicated by a minus) or needs to be specified in every sentence (indicated by a plus). In Arabic this is indicated by the initial *l-* of the word and in English by a separate word *the.* (Note in Table V that in Turkish definiteness is expressed for *water* but not in Table III for *boy;* this is because in Turkish definiteness is only indicated in the objective case.)

Column 6 in Table III refers to word order. Thus the number "2" for Arabic means that the word for *boy* is the second item in the sample sentence.

In Table IV, column 2 refers to verb tense, i.e., whether or not there is a formal indication of the time of the action. In Thai the form of the verb does not indicate the time of the action, hence the minus; however, if it were necessary to indicate it, it would be indicated by an additional word. In the other six languages the verb form does indicate completion, hence the plus signs.

Column 3 in Table IV refers to whether or not the verb form indicates that the action of drinking was carried through to completion. For example, in English if the action were described as continuing but as yet not finished, one would have to write "the boy was drinking . . ." In Russian, the prefix *vy-* indicates completion; "was drinking" would be *pil,* without this prefix. The plus signs show that completion of action is indicated by the verb in all seven languages.

Column 4 in Table IV refers to grammatical agreement in gender, person, and number between the subject noun *boy* and the verb *drank.* For example, Russian shows agreement in gender and number; if the subject had been feminine singular the verb would have been *výpila* while if the subject had been plural in either gender the verb would have been *výpili.*

Agreement in person refers, of course, to the distinction between first, second, and third person. In Arabic, for example, if the subject was the first person singular *I drank*, the form of the verb would be *šaráb-tu* 'I drank'.

Since the categories in Table V, of the object, *the water*, are the same as those of Table III, they do not have to be explained again. The only difference is that, as noted earlier, in Turkish definiteness is expressed for the object, not the subject.

However, the bases for the divisions of words by hyphens do need explanation. In Table III, in Arabic, *l-* is the definite article, *-u* indicates the nominative case, and the remainder, *-wálad-*, is the root for *boy*. The Thai word for *boy* is a compound of *dèg-* 'child' and *chaaj* 'masculine'.

In Table IV, in Russian, *vý-pi-l*, *vý-* indicates completion, *-l* indicates past, masculine, singular, while *-pi-* is the root for *to drink*. In Turkish, *iç-* is the root for *to drink* and *-tí* indicates past completion in the third person singular. In Arabic, *-a* indicates past completion, masculine, third person singular. In Hausa *yâ-* indicates third person, masculine, past completion, singular. In Quechua, *upiá-* is the root *to drink*, *-rqa-* is past completion, and *-n* indicates the third person singular.

In Table V, in Russian, *vód-u*, *-u* indicates the objective case. In Turkish *-yú* marks the definite object. In Arabic *l-* is the definite article and *-a* the objective case. In Quechua *-ta*, shows that the noun "water" is in the objective case.

Taking these tables as a whole, the diversity is immediately apparent. Where then are the common features?

To begin with, it is remarkable in a way that tables are possible at all. There exists a vast range of everyday situations which can be expressed in all languages of the world. Beyond this, there may be technical terms or terms for peculiar social institutions which have no simple translation equivalences; in principle, however, these can be explained in other languages and a new term introduced if necessary.

However, the common properties of these tables goes well beyond the fact of mere translatability. In all six non-English languages the three lexical items *boy*, *drink*, and *water* exist and have been used to translate the base sentence. In general, there is a large area of "fundamental vocabulary" of this kind found in all languages of the world.

All languages distinguish nouns and verbs either formally by differing grammatical inflections or by a fixed difference of word order or by both.

Further, the categories that are grammatically marked are few. Thus the addition of literally hundreds of languages, even of all the world's languages, will add very few grammatical categories which must be expressed in this particular sentence.

Besides the noun/verb distinction, all the languages indicate in an unambiguous way the grammatical relations of subject and object either by an overt case marker in the noun or by a fixed word order.

On the phonological side, all the languages in the sample (except Hausa, which is tonal and uses distinctions in pitch), mark the distinctness and integrity of the three categories involved, which are generally called "words." One method used is stress or accent. English, Turkish, Classical Arabic, Russian, and Quechua each have a single phonetically most heavily stressed syllable in each of the basic words. In Turkish it is practically always on the final syllable; in Quechua on the next to the last; in Arabic on the next to the last syllable if this syllable is long (has a consonant after the vowel or if the vowel is long), otherwise on the syllable before that if the word has at least three syllables. In Thai, which is also tonal, most words have a single syllable. Where, as in the word for *boy*, there are two syllables, the fact that it is a single word is marked by the closer junction of the two syllables so that the total temporal duration of the two syllables is less than if the sequence consisted of two words. Even Hausa marks word boundaries by shortening a vowel if it is at the end of a word. The word then is a universal unit in languages.

A further characteristic does not appear in the table. All the languages in some way mark that the three items together form a single unit, the sentence. This is accomplished by the regulation of pitch as distributed over the sentence, which is known as intonation. Moreover, in this type of sentence, which is a statement rather than a question, there is generally a fall in pitch which is greatest toward the end of the sentence. Indeed, it is always the end rather than the beginning that is the subject of the rule. Questions will generally be marked either by a rise in pitch at the end or a specific question word or a combination of the two. In other words, the sentence, like the word, is a universal unit and so is also classified into basic types such as "statements" and "questions."

Finally, even though the order of these units differs from language to language, there is almost always a normal order which is sometimes the only possible order. When there is variation, deviations from the normal order can occur to express differences in emphasis. We may define basic word order regarding subject noun, verb, and object noun as that which is usual in main clauses of declarative sentences. In a large majority of languages there is one "normal" order in the sense that it is the most frequently occurring and the most neutral in meaning. Specific deviations occur under special circumstances, e.g., for contrastive emphasis as in English COFFEE *I drink, but* TEA *I don't.*

These properties are, in general, found in all languages. Such universals may be called "unrestricted universals." Beyond this, however, a more careful examination of the differences themselves will reveal other, more subtle universal principles at work.

Consider, for example, the order of the three elements subject noun, verb, and object noun, symbolized as (1) S, (2) V, and (3) O, respectively. Of the languages considered here English, Russian, Hausa, and Thai have the order SVO; Turkish and Quechua have the order SOV, while Arabic has the order VSO. For these three elements six orders are theoretically possible, VSO, VOS, SOV, SVO, OVS, and OSV. Of these, the three found in the present examples will account for perhaps 99 per cent of the world's languages. A few others have the VOS order (e.g., Malagasy, the language of Madagascar) but the other two—OVS and OSV—are not known to occur anywhere.

The kind of classification of the world's language that this implies is known as "typology." Each of the six alternatives represents a theoretically possible type of language. Whenever one or more of these types does not exist, we have some sort of limitations on the possible kinds of human language, for which limitations there must be a universally valid reason.

The three most common types—SVO, SOV, and VSO—differ only in the placement of the verb. What they have in common is that the subject of the verb precedes its object. The only type occurring in which O precedes S is VOS.

This example of word order illustrates the point that even where there are differences, a closer examination in terms of types will show that these differences are not random but embody linguistic principles of universal validity.

Another case where apparent differences may mask linguistic principles of universal validity is the agreement between subject and verb (Table IV, column 4). We see among the seven languages no less than four possibilities: no agreement; agreement in gender and number; agreement in person and number; agreement in gender, person, and number. Offhand, this would seem to be unpromising material for generalization.

However, first we had no column for agreement with object. Where there is agreement between verb and noun, the verb almost invariably agrees with the subject, reflecting once more the fundamental nature of the subject-predicate division. Agreement functions as a kind of external mark of the relation between the subject and predicate. The predicate is represented by the verb probably because the verb is the most fundamental element in the predicate. With intransitive verbs, e.g., *she walks*, the predicate is represented solely by the verb.

There are a very few languages in the world in which the verb agrees with the object. This agreement is necessarily confined to the transitive verb since the intransitive verb by definition has no object. Languages that have object agreement belong to a particular type in which it is possible to show that what looks like a transitive active construction actually is a passive construction that has been generalized. If, in any language, in a sentence like "the boy drank water," *drink* agrees with *water* rather than *boy* in gender and/or number, this turns out to be because the agreement originated from, or should even be analyzed at present as, the passive construction "the water was drunk by the boy," in which, of course, *water* is actually the subject and not the object.

In the languages that have subject-verb agreement in our sentence, adjectives and other modifiers of the noun also agree with the noun in gender and number. Person is a different kind of category since it is not usually exhibited in the noun as such. Nouns in general are third person while only the pronouns may have forms in all three persons. Verbs may then vary depending on the person of the subject since the subject may be a pronoun or a noun. For example, in Russian, in which the verb in our sentence agrees with the subject in gender and number, the adjective also agrees with the noun in this category.

For Russian there is an additional relevant fact that does not appear from the sentence given in the table. It is only in the past tense that the Russian verb agrees with the subject in gender. In the present, for example, the noun subject agrees in person and number, but not in gender. Once more, history is enlightening. The Russian past is historically a participle, i.e., an adjective derived from the verb, meaning *having drunk* or the like and was formerly used with the verb *to be*. Thus "the boy drank" was formerly "the boy was a having-drunk [person]," as it were. In some other Slavic languages this use of the verb *to be* is still the case.

What this suggests is that gender agreement is in some sense more fundamental between noun and adjective than between subject noun and verb. This is confirmed in many languages that do not appear in our tables. For example, in French the noun and modifying adjective agree in gender and number, but the noun agrees with the verb in number only.

Even what are at first glance idiosyncratic rules can sometimes be shown to illustrate general principles. It was noted that in Turkish there was a different case form for the object, though not the subject, depending upon whether it was definite or not. In our example *the water* as object was *su-yú*. If the meaning had been *the boy drank water*, the object would have been *su*. Other languages, for example, Persian, have this same peculiarity of distinguishing definiteness in the object of the verb but not in the subject. On the other hand no language is known to make this distinction in the subject without making it in the object. This leads to what is generally called an "implicational universal" in contrast to the unrestricted universal mentioned earlier. Whenever a language expresses grammatically the difference between definiteness in the subject, it always does so in the object.

The reason for this is probably that the subject of the sentence is likely to be something we have talked about before and may therefore be assumed to be definite. Some languages only allow definite subjects. This is less likely to be so for the object. Hence, some languages mark this distinction for the object by an affix. The indefinite object in such language has no affix and coincides in form with the subject. Further cross-linguistic comparison of this one sentence would yield several other general principles.

Work along these lines is now proceeding actively, revealing a panhuman set of preferences which are either absolute where the universals are unrestricted or among sets of alternatives. We seek the general principles which will explain these specific generalizations. Even the limited sample discussed here shows that some of these are beginning to emerge. Given language's uniqueness and centrality to man and its vast complexity, such principles should provide basic insights into the functioning of the human mind. Chomsky and the transformationalist school have emphasized the complexity and richness of innate endowment which man must have to construct languages. However, a central point of contention, even within the transformational school, is whether this endowment is specifically linguistic and involves a kind of genetic programming for the over-all universal features of grammars or whether it involves more general inherited faculties which display themselves both in nonlinguistic and linguistic behavior.

The typological approach, which could only be sketched in bare outline in the present chapter, appears to be producing results which supplement those of the transformational approach. The existence of conditional hierarchical preferences suggests particularly that the second alternative is more likely to be correct. That is, what is built in is rather a general set of psychological and physiological (in the case of phonetics) preferences of a highly general nature rather than the specific form of grammars. How these work out then in specific languages depends on given historical, social, and cultural factors.

Whatever the final truth in this matter, the study of language universals, which is being pursued from several points of view, is producing exciting and important results that should contribute in a basic way to our understanding of human nature.

APPENDIX A

Phonetic Symbols

æ = *a* in *cat*
ɛ = *e* in *end*
ɪ = *i* in *it*
i = *e* in *eve*
ʊ = *u* in *pull*
u = *oo* in *ooze*
aj = *ie* in *tie*
aw = *ou* in *house*
ə = *a* in *sofa*
č = *ch* in *church*
j = *j* in *judge*
š = *sh* in *shawl*
y = *y* in *yes*
ž = *z* in *azure*
θ = *th* in *thin*
ð = *th* in *that*
ŋ = *ng* in *sing*
: = vowel length
ʻ = aspiration
= = unreleased stop

APPENDIX B

The English Consonants—Place and Manner of Articulation

	Bilabial	Labio-dental	Dental	Alveolar	Palatal	Velar	Glottal
STOPS	p b			t d		k g	
FRICATIVES		f v	θ ð	s z	š ž		h*
AFFRICATES					č ǰ		
NASALS	m			n		ŋ	
LATERAL				l			
SEMIVOWELS	w†			r	y		

* Classed as a fricative on the basis of acoustic effect. It sounds more or less like [fθs], even though it is like a vowel without voice.

† [w] is velar as well as bilabial, since the back of the tongue is raised as it is for [u].

From D. Bolinger, *Aspects of Language*, 2d ed. (New York: Harcourt Brace Jovanovich, 1975).

SELECTED READINGS

General

Bolinger, Dwight Le Merton. *Aspects of Language*. 2d ed. New York: Harcourt Brace Jovanovich, 1975.

Langacker, Ronald W. *Language and Its Structure*. New York: Harcourt, Brace & World, 1968.

Lyons, John. *Introduction to Theoretical Linguistics*. London: Cambridge University Press, 1968.

Histories of Linguistics

Hymes, Dell H., ed. *Studies in the History of Linguistics: Traditions and Paradigms*. Bloomington: Indiana University Press, 1974.

Robins, Robert H. *A Short History of Linguistics*. Bloomington: Indiana University Press, 1968.

Phonetics and Phonology

Abercrombie, David. *Elements of General Phonetics*. Edinburgh: University of Edinburgh Press, 1967.

Brosnahan, Leonard Francis, and Bertil Malmberg. *Introduction to Phonetics*. Cambridge, England: Heffer, 1970.

Hyman, Larry M. *Phonology: Theory and Analysis*. New York: Holt, Rinehart and Winston, 1975.

Ladefoged, Peter. *A Course in Phonetics*. New York: Harcourt Brace Jovanovich, 1975.

Language and Culture

Burling, Robbins. *Man's Many Voices: Language in Its Cultural Context*. New York: Holt, Rinehart and Winston, 1970.

Hoijer, Harry, ed. *Language in Culture: Conference on the Interrelation of Language and Other Aspects of Culture*. Chicago: University of Chicago Press, 1954.

Hymes, Dell H., ed. *Language in Culture and Society: A Reader in Linguistics and Anthropology.* New York: Harper & Row, 1964.

Whorf, Benjamin L. *Language, Thought and Reality: Selected Writings of Benjamin Lee Whorf.* Ed. by John B. Carroll. Cambridge, Mass.: Technology Press Book, Massachusetts Institute of Technology, 1956.

Sociolinguistics

Fishman, Joshua A. *Sociolinguistics: A Brief Introduction.* Rowley, Mass.: Newbury House, 1970.

Gumperz, John T. *Language in Social Groups.* Stanford, Cal.: Stanford University Press, 1971.

Key, Marie Ritchie. *Male/Female Language, with a Comprehensive Bibliography.* Metuchen, N.J.: Scarecrow Press, 1975.

Labov, William. *Sociolinguistic Patterns.* Philadelphia: University of Pennsylvania Press, 1973.

Psycholinguistics

Brown, Roger. *Psycholinguistics: Selected Papers by Roger Brown.* New York: Free Press, 1970.

Clark, Herbert H. and Eve V. *Psychology and Language: An Introduction to Psycholinguistics.* New York: Harcourt Brace Jovanovich, 1977.

Fodor, J. A., T. G. Bever, and M. F. Garrett. *The Psychology of Language: An Introduction to Psycholinguistics and Generative Grammar.* New York: McGraw-Hill, 1974.

Historical Linguistics

Anttila, Raimo. *An Introduction to Historical and Comparative Linguistics.* New York: Macmillan, 1972.

King, Robert Desmond. *Historical Linguistics and Generative Grammar.* Englewood Cliffs, N.J.: Prentice-Hall, 1969.

Lehmann, Winfred Philipp. *Historical Linguistics: An Introduction.* 2d ed. New York: Holt, Rinehart and Winston, 1973.

Language Universals

Greenberg, Joseph H., ed. *Universals of Language.* 2d ed. Cambridge, Mass.: Cambridge University Press, 1966.

INDEX